Discovering the
MOORS AND DALES
OF THE PEAK DISTRICT

Words by Jerry Rawson and Roger Redfern
Photographs by Jerry Rawson

HALSGROVE

First published in 2002 by Halsgrove
Text © 2002 Jerry Rawson and Roger Redfern
Images © 2002 Jerry Rawson

British Library Cataloguing-in-Publication Data
A CIP record for this title is available from the British Library

ISBN 1 84114 194 1

HALSGROVE

Halsgrove House
Lower Moor Way
Tiverton, Devon EX16 6SS
Tel: 01884 243242
Fax: 01884 243325
email: sales@halsgrove.com
website: www.halsgrove.com

Printed and bound in Italy
by Centro Grafico Ambrosiano

CONTENTS

Eroded gritstone boulders at Ramshaw Rocks.

WALK LOCATIONS

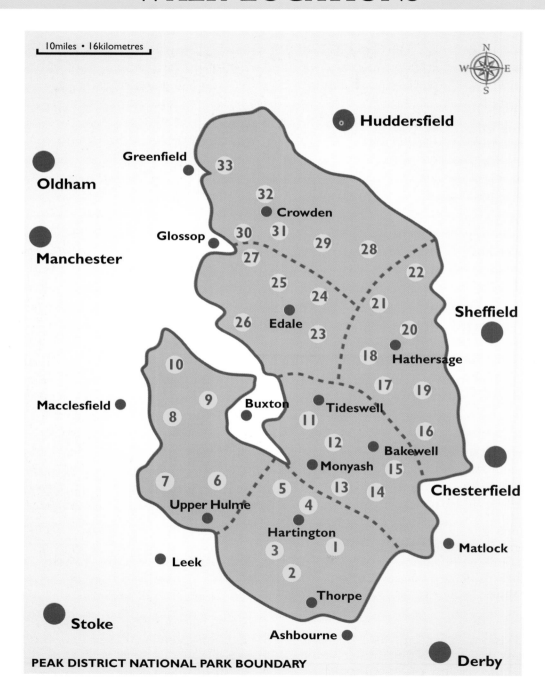

INTRODUCTION

If you like tramping across wild, heather moorland; or following river courses through beautiful wooded dales; or exploring villages along with their industrial and archaeological history; or simply enjoy looking at stunning landscapes, then the Peak District has it all, and much more.

The 555 square miles (1438 square km) of the Peak District National Park, the first to be designated way back in 1951, is a diverse area of gritstone moorlands and gentle rolling limestone pastureland interspersed with small towns and villages. Set at the southern end of the Pennine Chain, the Peak District forms a marked transition between the lowlands and the uplands. This sharp division can best be seen when looking westwards from the summit of Shutlingsloe across the Cheshire Plain or southwards from the Roaches escarpment towards the patchwork fields around Leek and beyond to the Potteries.

The area consists of two clearly defined types of scenery, produced by different rocks – millstone grit and limestone. The high moorland plateaux of Kinder Scout, Bleaklow and Black Hill, are a mixture of heather, peat and eroded gritstone tors, and along with the western moors of Axe Edge and the eastern moors stretching above the villages of Hathersage and Baslow with their famous gritstone edges, form a horseshoe shape covering about three quarters of the total area, which is known as the Dark Peak.

Enclosed within this inverted 'U' is the rolling limestone area of the White Peak, formed when the area was under a tropical sea near the equator. Laid down during the Carboniferous period more than 350

Hen Cloud and the Roaches escarpment.

million years ago, the limestone is made up the remains of microscopic sea creatures. On the edges of the tropical lagoons harder reef limestones were deposited to produce the few real peaks in the Peak District, such as Chrome and Parkhouse Hills in the Upper Dove Valley.

Walkers on Kinder Scout.

The end of a perfect day on Kinder Scout.

Tissington Spires, Dovedale.

This undulating limestone tableland is criss-crossed by an intricate pattern of miles of drystone walls and split by deeply-cut, wooded dales. Some of the valleys contain rivers notably the Lathkill, Hamps and Manifold that in summer disappear underground only to reappear some distance downstream, while others, like Dovedale, contain spectacular pinnacles, crags and caves. These limestone dales are havens for wildlife and you will also find a tremendous range of wild flowers here.

Springtime in Wolfscote Dale.

The millstone grit of the Dark Peak landscape was formed from river-borne sands and gravels which were deposited on top of the Carboniferous limestone. Gigantic movements and contortions of the Earth's crust formed a massive dome and over aeons of time the shales and grits were eroded away to expose the older and deeper limestone below. The awesome power of Ice Age glaciers and their fast flowing meltwater rivers finally created many of the features of the Peak District we recognise today. Unlike the well-drained limestone landscape, the scenery of the Dark Peak is dominated by areas of poorly drained peat and heather moorland cut by deep drainage channels known as 'groughs'. On these moors are to be found birds like curlew and the ubiquitous red grouse, whose familiar 'go-back, go-back' call will accompany you on many moorland walks.

Surrounded by the conurbations of Manchester, Sheffield and the Midlands, it is not surprising that the Peak District has provided an escape, a playground for walkers, rock climbers, cyclists and cavers. Despite the relatively small area, the Peak provides a range of diverse walks. and although rarely rising over 610m/2000ft above sea level these hills have played a major role in the development of hill walking as a recreational activity. As far back as the end of the nineteenth century the moors of the Dark Peak attracted 'Bogtrotters', as they became known, who left a legacy of tough walks which still offer challenges to their modern counterparts. One of these, the Edale to Marsden trek which crosses Black Hill, Bleaklow and Kinder Scout, still demands respect, especially in bad weather conditions, a hundred years after its conception.

In those early days, much of the high ground was preserved grouse moors jealously guarded by gamekeepers and rights of access were virtually non-existent. Today, after numerous battles, physical and legal, there is almost unrestricted access to much of the Peak District moorlands. Historically, Kinder Scout has played a major role in gaining access to open moorlands culminating in the famous 1932 mass trespass. The event was a milestone in the fight for access to open country and helped speed up the Access to Mountains Act 1939, and more significantly, the National Parks and Access to the Countryside Act 1949 and the eventual formation of the Peak District National Park in 1951. It is

hoped that the few large tracts of moorland that still remain closed to walkers will become accessible with the implementation of the Countryside and Rights of Way Act 2000, which will give greater freedom to explore mapped areas of access land.

Above: *Frozen peat makes for easy walking across Kinder Scout.*

Sheep have helped to create the moorland landscape.

Left: *A Bleaklow wilderness.*

8

The main criteria for selection of walks for this book was that they were enjoyable, challenging and also reflected the many varied facets of the Peak – its people, its history and its working landscape – and would help first time visitors to experience some of the most magnificent scenery the area has to offer. For regular walkers maybe the selection will rekindle happy memories of days spent on the hills and might even offer a few undiscovered gems. By grouping the excursions into six reasonably well-defined geographical areas, it means that a trip to any one will give a choice of several walks, often from the same base.

The Moat Stone, Kinder Scout.

Each walk is circular and the text is merely used to 'whet the appetite' for a particular area. With the relevant maps, and a little imagination, the walks can be modified to suit individual tastes and abilities. There are alternative starting points for many of the walks and the times given for the routes are only a general guideline and assume the walk will be undertaken in reasonable weather conditions. Giving a walk a grade is very subjective and depends on many factors such as fitness level, navigation skills, experience, age, weather etc., but we have tried to indicate the relative seriousness of the walk by grading it easy, moderate, difficult or very difficult. The grade given on the information panels is based on terrain, height ascended and total distance covered.

The selected walks range from easy riverside strolls through wooded, limestone valleys, to demanding expeditions over wild moorland terrain where higher fitness levels and map and compass skills are essential, especially in bad weather when low clouds can cover the moors. In winter conditions the featureless and inhospitable parts of the Dark Peak can be very unforgiving for the ill-prepared walker, and the terrain demands the same respect as the higher hills of the Lake District and Snowdonia. However, in fine frosty weather when the peat is frozen rock hard the moors can provide magical days which live in the memory forever.

Most of the starting points for the walks are accessible by public transport including good rail access to Buxton, Edale and the Hope Valley from Manchester and Sheffield and a network of bus routes. For details use the National Traveline Tel: 0870 608 2608 or www.derbybus.net or www.pti.org.uk.

Crowden Clough, Kinder Scout – one of the classic approaches to the plateau.

A wide range of accommodation is available including hotels, guest houses, B&Bs, camping, camping barns and youth hostels (Tel: 01629 582983 or www.yha.org.uk) For details use www.peakdistrict-tourism.gov.uk and www.cressbrook.co.uk.

Tourist information is available at various Peak District National Park Information Centres including the Park headquarters at Bakewell Tel: 01629 816200 and www.peakdistrict.org.

No matter how often people visit the Peak District, and whatever the weather, the area always seems to provide something new to draw walkers back time and time again. In the enthusiastic words of Lord Byron, 'There are prospects in Derbyshire as noble as any in Greece or Switzerland'. But, of course, large parts of the Peak District lie in Cheshire, Staffordshire, South Yorkshire and Greater Manchester. We hope you have as much pleasure as we had in discovering these Peakland prospects.

Jerry Rawson and Roger Redfern

Top: *Early purple orchids in upper Cressbrook Dale.*

Above: *Limestone walls marching across the White Peak.*

Ladybower Reservoir and the Derwent Valley.

A Brief History of the Peak District

Few places in Britain have such a fascinating history as the Peak District, and, for walkers who journey over the hills or down the dales, some knowledge of this interesting past can add an extra dimension to the day out. Very little is known of the primitive people who first occupied Peakland, but they left behind artifacts and structures throughout the landscape, which have provided clues in fitting together this fascinating and complex story of the area's heritage.

After the last Ice Age nomadic hunters came into the district on hunting trips, following the migrating herds of animals which provided food and clothing. These early hunters used the many limestone caves in the dry valleys and gorges as shelters which have since provided the first traces of Stone Age occupation. The occupiers of Thor's Cave in the Manifold Valley left a multitude of simple artifacts in the floor soil, but crude Victorian excavations provided little information about how those cave dwellers lived. Not all cave diggings were so badly done however, and the adjacent Elderbush Cave for example, gave up its valuable secrets between 1935 and 1952. Also the nearby cave at the foot of Dowel Dale in the Upper Dove Valley and the rock shelter at Sheldon have also confirmed the presence of early habitation, so we now know more of the vegetation, fauna and the life styles of people in the last glacial period.

As the climate of Britain changed again about 10,000 years ago, forests began to replace the open, tundra-like terrain and the thick layers of blanket bog that now covers the gritstone moors began to form. Remnants of such primeval forests can still be found in the peat today. This wooded terrain attracted groups of hunter-gatherers in small communities and numerous flint tools of this Mesolithic (Middle Stone Age) period have been discovered. With a plentiful supply of food, and with a warmer and drier climate, colonization of the northern areas began to occur and an almost idyllic lifestyle existed.

There was a gradual transition from the hunter-gatherers to the Neolithic (New Stone Age) farmers at around 3000BC. These early settlers became builders and constructed stone chambers to inter their dead. At least nine of these Neolithic chambered tombs have been dis-

covered in the White Peak, notably at Five Wells near Taddington. The settlement pattern of that period was concentrated on the limestone plateau, probably due to the greater fertility of the land. However, the greatest relics from that period are the henge monuments of the 48m(160ft) diameter recumbent stone circle of Arbor Low, between Parsley Hay and Youlgreave, and the now-stoneless Bull Ring near Dove Holes. The reason for building these structures still remain a mystery but they are fascinating places to explore. Historians used to believe that Stone Age settlements only existed on the limestone plateau, but excavations on the moors at Gardom's Edge above Baslow have revealed a large defended enclosure dating from the Neolithic period, thought to be the largest of its kind in Northern England.

Top: *Looking out of Thor's Cave in the Manifold Valley to Wetton Hill. The cave provided shelter for Stone Age people 5000 years ago.*

Above: *The Five Wells Neolithic chambered tomb overlooking the Wye Valley.*

The fallen stones of Arbor Low, near Parsley Hay.

The Nine Ladies stone circle dating from the Bronze Age.

Development in metal working techniques led to the Bronze Age and, along with the Neolithic Period, lasted for at least 2000 years leaving a marked impact on the landscape. Stanton Moor is one of the richest areas for relics during this period with stone circles, barrows, standing stones and cairns. It was once written that 'Stanton Moor is as thick with tumuli as a plum duff with raisins'. Early Bronze Age inhabitants from about 2000BC are often known as Beaker People from the small bronze vessels that have been excavated from graves. Burial customs also altered; chambered tombs were no longer used, instead a mound of earth was placed over the burial place forming a round barrow. Many of these have been found in the limestone country. Around 1000BC the custom of cremation was introduced and Stanton Moor has yielded more than fifteen urns in which ashes were buried.

Sadly the building of enclosure walls led to the destruction of many Bronze Age burial sites, so only a fragmented record of the Peak's prehistory has survived until modern times. However, there is evidence to show that in the later Bronze Age times there were settlements on the gritstone uplands east of the Derwent Valley.

The Bronze Age slowly moved into the Iron Age around 500BC but few artifacts have been found from that period. However, the main feature from that time are the string of hill forts which encircle prominent hills of which the most impressive is the ditch and rampart on Mam Tor overlooking the head of the Hope Valley. Others include Castle Naze above Chapel-en-le-Frith and Fin Cop overlooking Monsal Dale.

The Romans came to Peakland about 80AD and have left their mark with a network of roads which connected several forts. The tribe of people known as Brigantes, struggled against this occupying force but were eventually defeated. This period also marks the transition from prehistory to recorded history for the Romans left us a legacy of written information. At the heart of the district was the fort at Navio, near Brough, probably the administrative centre in those days, which was connected with the fort of Melandra near Glossop, and the thermal baths of Aquae Arnemetiae at Buxton. Roman Peakland appears to have been a relatively settled time with lead mining and farming being the main occupations.

After the departure of the Romans they were replaced around 400AD by the Saxons and Angles, which marked the start of an unsettled period of warring between Pagan and Christian groups. This period became known as the Dark Ages and crosses in the churchyards at Eyam, Hope and Bakewell belong to this time. Also the Saxon tribe of the Pecsaetan gave us the name Peak District while the Vikings, who eventually took much of the area, also had an impact on some place names with the Odin Mine at Castleton and the village of Rowland dating from those times. During this period the stone villages and farming communities, which are so characteristic of the White Peak were set up.

When the Normans arrived on the scene the dominant feature of the landscape were the vast areas of open country that were quickly taken over by the great Norman families and turned into hunting parks. The most impressive of these was the Royal Forest of the Peak, which occupied 40 square miles of the northern section, and Macclesfield Forest to the west. Although hunting was the paramount activity at that time, exploitation of the ground for lead and other minerals was also important. Eventually the medieval landscape became denuded of much of its glorious tree cover.

The administration of the Royal Forest of the Peak was from Peveril Castle, the only stone castle in the area and it dominated Castleton. It has been called the finest medieval landmark in the district and received its first mention in the Domesday Book. Another outstanding castle mound is Bailey Hill behind Bradfield parish church, which was one of the best-fortified sites for miles. It is topped by trees now but in Norman times would have supported a wooden motte and bailey castle.

During the Middle Ages powerful monastic establishments acquired large areas of land to provide food and extra income; Welbeck Abbey, for example, owned an estate in Upper Derwent Dale. Distributed across the limestone plateau are large farms or 'granges' once owned by powerful religious houses still exist; One Ash Grange, south of Lathkill Dale, was owned by Roche Abbey and still retains the feel of a large medieval holding.

The White Peak as a whole constitutes an important source of minerals so that mining has formed an important activity with the ensuing scars of old mine workings, spoil heaps and rakes now forming a characteristic part of the landscape. Lead mining has been carried on since Roman times, forming much of the wealth of the Peak District for more than 1500 years. The industry that once brought employment and prosperity and gave rise to the growth of settlements like Wirksworth is now defunct. Many of the old workings, largely confined to the limestone tableland, now provide interest for industrial archaeologists and potholers. Some of the larger rakes are visible for miles and are often characterized by their tree-lined rim that prevented grazing animals eating contaminated grass.

Castle Naze, site of an Iron Age fort overlooking Chapel-en-le-Frith.

The next important development in the chequered history of the Peak District was the Industrial Revolution which came quite early to some parts. Richard Arkwright set up his cotton mill at Cromford in 1771 making the first successful application of water power, maybe the first mechanised textile mill in the world. From medieval times the main transport for Peakland products was packhorse trains and horse and cart. Many of the ancient routes across the area have been used since Roman times and certainly some date from pre-history. These old ways were often adapted as routes for turnpike roads about the middle of the eighteenth century. Transport methods soon changed dramatically with the advent of the Railway Age which brought great activity to the hills – from the armies of navvies driving the Woodhead Tunnel beneath the high moors between the Don and the Etherow, to the opening of the Midland Railway route through the Wye Valley in 1863. The Hope Valley line (1894), incidentally, opened up hitherto inaccessible areas to ramblers. Edale, for example, owed much of its popularity with early ramblers to this Sheffield-Manchester link.

More than anything else though, it was the wholesale enclosure of great areas of the district in the eighteenth and nineteenth centuries that changed the face of the countryside which we explore today. Hordes of labourers constructed mile upon mile of drystone walls around the newly created fields upon the limestone tableland and across the gritstone and shale uplands. Apart from the industrial scars created by limestone quarrying, the face of the Peak District has changed little since those days. The field patterns that give so much pleasure to the eye were built when labour was cheap. Many of the walls have now reached the end of their useful lives but while they last they add magic line and perspective to a still evolving landscape.

Gardom's Edge above Baslow where excavations have revealed a defended enclosure dating from Neolithic times.

Magpie Mine.

Barn and walled fields near Sheldon.

14

Saxon cross in Eyam churchyard.

An ancient packhorse bridge over the River Bradford near Youlgreave.

Preserved pattern of strip fields at Chelmorton.

Seventeenth-century Eyam Hall.

The Manifold and Dove

Although the courses of the Dove and Manifold Rivers are only a few kilometres apart and run parallel from their sources on the gritstone moors at Axe Edge, near Buxton, to their confluence at Ilam, 20km/12miles to the south, they have formed very different types of valleys. Whereas the young Dove flows gently past shapely reef limestone hills before rushing through deeply cut, narrow gorges with dramatic rock scenery, the Manifold pursues a more tranquil course, especially south of Hulme End. Where the meandering river flows through a deep but broad limestone valley with wooded hillsides, overlooked by the citadel of Thor's Cave.

In the distant geological past, shale and gritstone layers covered this limestone plateau through which the Dove and Manifold have flowed. The rivers, swollen by meltwater from Ice Age glaciers, etched deeply into the bedded limestone, taking advantage of underground passages, which made this process so much easier. The harder reef limestone crags and pinnacles were left dotted along the valley sides. Considerable time has elapsed since any subterranean river has carved out Dovedale whereas in the Manifold Valley this action is still going on, albeit slowly. In dry weather much of the River Manifold disappears underground to reappear near Ilam. Eventually this extensive network of caves and passages may collapse creating a much deeper and more spectacular defile than Dovedale. Just try to picture it!

South of Hulme End the Manifold is shadowed by a tarmaced track which follows the course of the former Leek and Manifold Light Railway, built in 1898 to carry freight and tourists along the Manifold and Hamps valleys to the railhead at Waterhouses, but closed in 1934. The track is now very popular with walkers and cyclists.

Some of the most beautiful plants in the Peak District are to be found in these valleys and Dovedale's naturally-regenerating ash woods are of national importance. Thankfully, most of Dovedale with its spectacular limestone crags are in the safe hands of the National Trust.

These popular valleys have long ranked as a bastion of romantic scenery attracting painters, writers and poets. It was Alfred Lord Tennyson who described Dovedale as 'one of the most unique and delicious places in England.' Another appealing feature of this area are the scattered stone villages, many having a rugged and distinctive character set in a breezy landscape. Down the centuries their surrounding uplands, criss-crossed by miles of drystone walls, have been influenced and colonized by various groups from prehistoric cave dwellers, through the Dark Ages, right up to the present time. Evidence of these historical influences around the Dove and Manifold can be clearly seen during the following walks.

Above: *Manifold Valley from Thor's Cave.*

Right: *The limestone buttresses of Dovedale Church.*

WALK 1 — A Tour of the Dove

Downstream from the upland village of Hartington, the Dove gurgles its way along peaceful Beresford and Wolfscote Dales, before passing through rugged Milldale and Dovedale to its confluence with the River Manifold near Ilam. Acting as a natural boundary dividing Derbyshire and Staffordshire, this almost continuous gorge stretching from Hartington to Thorpe contains some of the most beautiful dales scenery in the White Peak. William Adam in his nineteenth century *Gem of the Peak*, said that 'to make a tour of the Dove is a matter of course to all who come to admire and enjoy the wonders of the Peak'. These are sentiments that still hold true today.

Starting from Hartington, this circular walk visits both counties, explores the breezy landscape of the surrounding uplands and takes in some of the less well-known side dales.

Hartington, with its old stone houses, was once the hub of a thriving agricultural area and also had links with lead and copper mining. Recorded in the Domesday survey of 1086, Hartington was granted a market charter in 1203, the oldest in the Peak District, and it still maintains the open area – along with a pond – where the market used to be held. Apart from tourism, nowadays the main village industry is the cheese factory, located just off the village green. The village has some exquisite buildings including the parish church of St Giles, with its Perpendicular tower dating from the early thirteenth century, while in a secluded spot on the hill opposite, stands Hartington Hall, a superb example of seventeenth-century Peakland vernacular architecture with stone mullioned windows. Built by the Bateman family in 1611, the hall has been a popular youth hostel since the 1930s.

Thorpe Cloud, Dovedale.

Hartington to Alstonefield

From just along the Warslow (B5054) road a footpath crosses walled fields and meadows down to wooded Beresford Dale, where a rustic wooden bridge crosses the Dove from Derbyshire into Staffordshire. Ahead lies a craggy wooded gorge containing Pike Pool, with its spire-like rock leaping from the water, which is forever associated with the seventeenth-century duo of Charles Cotton and his friend Izaak Walton who extolled the virtues of the place in their classic 1653 publication, *The Compleat Angler*. Here was Cotton's 'beloved Nymph, fair Dove, Princess of rivers...' Walton even built a fishing temple nearby.

Beyond the pool, another narrow bridge takes you back into Derbyshire where grassy meadows are crossed to the simple 'v' shaped Wolfscote Dale overlooked on the left by two large limestone buttresses, one containing a cave known as Frank i'the Rocks. Evidence has been found here of both Roman and Anglo Saxon burials.

The wooded, closed-in atmosphere of Beresford Dale is in marked contrast with the open aspect of Wolfscote Dale consisting of steep slopes of grass and scree dotted with numerous limestone outcrops. Meadow sweet and celandine adorn the banks of the Dove and you might see the elusive dippers that frequent this part of the river as it scurries over numerous weirs. Eventually a junction with the dry valley of Biggin Dale is reached, its entrance overlooked by the cliffs of Drabber Tor and the craggy ribs of Peaseland Rocks.

Downstream from the junction, a footbridge spans the Dove from where steep grassy slopes are climbed up to the limestone plateau. Here, walled pastures lead up to the pretty village of Alstonefield with its green and fine church of St Peter, originally built in the twelfth century.

Ilam Rock, Dovedale.

Wolfscote Dale.

Cave, a natural cavern approached by an impressive arch, while a little further downstream is the group of pinnacles known as Tissington Spires. Just beyond here is Lover's Leap, from where you can look across the river to Dovedale Castle and the outcrops of the Twelve Apostles backed by the rare sight of naturally-regenerating ash woods.

The valley now begins to open up and gentle pastures lead to the famous Stepping Stones which cross the river at a narrow point hemmed in by the shapely sentinels of Thorpe Cloud and Bunster Hill. A slight detour up Thorpe Cloud or Bunster Hill provides great views up Dovedale.

Alstonefield to Dovedale

Just after leaving Alstonefield along the Wetton road, a walled lane, then a path descend across fields to the road through Hopedale. Straight ahead is the grassy Brunister Lane – lined with daffodils in springtime – leading up to the farming hamlet of Stanshope from where fields are crossed to the narrow confines of Hall Dale. This dry, craggy valley twists its way down below Hurt's Wood to the valley bottom. Here the scene is quite dramatic with the slender reef limestone fin of Ilam Rock rising from the water's edge like a discarded Easter Island monolith, while opposite, on the Derbyshire side is Pickering Tor, a natural tower.

The dale has been eulogised in books and poems, painted and photographed and as such needs little introduction to many walkers. There often seems to be a new delight around every corner of the dale.

After crossing the bridge beside Ilam Rock, the walk continues along the eastern banks of the Dove, passing Lion's Head Rock and Reynard's

Viator's Bridge, Milldale.

An autumn walk in Dovedale.

Dovedale to Milldale

This stage of the walk follows the rim of Dovedale's eastern slopes and provides an unusual perspective of some of the pinnacles passed earlier. Just upstream from the Stepping Stones, a path gradually slants up onto the Sharplow ridge and contours above the gorse scrubland from where fine views abound, especially down to Tissington Spires. As the path traverses around the head of Sharplow Dale, Hall Dale comes into view across the valley. At the head of tiny Pickering Dale these airy vistas are exchanged for a tunnel-like track slanting down Upper Taylor's Wood, landing you back at the Dove by the cave-like Dove Holes, which in summer look like two huge eyes peering through a green fringe.

Continuing alongside the Dove, past several impressive crags, Viator's Bridge and the hamlet of Milldale are soon reached. Nestling in the valley bottom, the hamlet derives its name from an old corn mill once situated here. The unusual name given to the packhorse bridge originates from a companion of Charles Cotton, named in *The Compleat Angler* as 'Viator', from the Latin word for traveller.

Milldale to Hartington

Rather than take the narrow road alongside the river to Wolfscote Dale, a more interesting way is to ascend the steep zigzags up the grassy slopes above the bridge to Hanson Toot. A toot was a lookout, and as you arrive here you certainly get an aerial view into Hopedale and Milldale. The path follows the crest of Shining Tor from where you can peer into Wolfscote Dale, whose entrance is approached by a narrow road joined just beyond the tor.

At first the dale is characterised by meadow pastures but these soon give way to a steep-sided valley through which the eastern side of the river is followed as the wooded dale twists and turns. The valley is rich in wild flowers, such as meadow cranesbill, thyme and the delicate rock rose, which grow profusely on the limestone rocks and screes.

Back at the junction with Biggin Dale the main valley is quitted for the last time up this quiet and open subsidiary valley into the Biggin Dale National Nature Reserve. In springtime the blackthorn with its white flowers puts on a great display. After a gentle climb, the dale opens up and our way lies leftwards along Reynard's Lane back into Hartington, with its welcoming tea shops and pubs.

Looking from Bunster Hill up Dovedale to Tissington Spires.

INFORMATION
Start/Finish: Hartington GR 128604.
Distance/Time: 26km(16miles) / 7hours.
Grading: Moderate; a long walk on lanes, tracks, field and valley footpaths.
Map: OS Outdoor Leisure sheet 24 White Peak Area.
Refreshments: The George Inn and tea rooms at Alstonefield; pubs and cafés in Hartington.
Public Transport: Regular bus service from Buxton and Ashbourne.

Marsh marigold growing on the banks of the Dove.

The steep-sided Wolfscote Dale.

Frank i'th'Rocks, Wolfscote Dale.

WALK 2 Ilam and Beeston Tor

Although much of the twisting Manifold Valley can be followed along the route of the old Leek and Manifold Light Railway, now a tarmaced track, the picturesque wooded section between Beeston Tor and Ilam is best appreciated from the surrounding heights on both sides of the valley. To discover the charms of this southern end of the Manifold this circular walk starts from the Staffordshire village of Ilam, traverses the eastern flanks of the valley that reveal a beautiful and unusual aspect of the area, returning via Throwley Hall on the western rim of the valley before descending the quiet wooded valley of Musden back to Ilam.

The pretty estate village of Ilam, a Saxon name meaning 'at the hills', is overlooked by the grassy slopes of Bunster Hill and has a fascinating history. Ilam's original village was moved from near Ilam Hall to its present location in the 1820s and rebuilt in the Alpine Style by the shipping magnate Jesse Watts Russell. The centre of the village is dominated by the imitation Eleanor Cross, built by Russell in memory of his first wife, Mary. He also rebuilt Ilam Hall, just to the west of the village, in a grand Gothic style. Set in a country park overlooked by steep grassy

Ilam Country Park.

slopes and hanging woods, what remains of Ilam Hall is now a National Trust property and youth hostel. The parish church just below the hall, has some interesting Saxon crosses in the churchyard and a shrine to the Saxon St Bertram, an eighth-century son of a Mercian king who renounced his heritage for religion.

Ilam Hall to Beeston Tor

From the village a road leads to the National Trust car park in front of Ilam Hall where signs point the way between the buildings and down steps through woodland to the river near the Manifold resurgence at Ilam Spring. This is the Boil Hole where the Manifold reappears after its 6km/4mile underground journey from near Wetton Mill. It shares this ability to go subterranean with the River Hamps, which also bubbles to the surface just upstream from here.

A pleasant riverside stroll leads through pastures and woodland to River Lodge at the narrow road from Ilam. The path passes beside the Battle Stone, a cross shaft found under a cottage during the rebuilding of Ilam village and is associated with the struggle between the Saxons and the Danes, probably dating from the middle of the eleventh century.

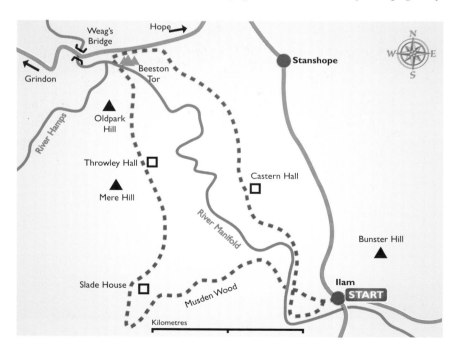

Ilam church backed by Bunster Hill.

Although there is no riverside path beyond River Lodge, the eastern rim of the valley provides a lovely walk with splendid views down into the densely wooded floor of the valley. Along the road left from River Lodge a lane branches rightwards up to Castern Hall, ancient seat of the Hurts. Beyond the farm buildings a path contours round the hillside and climbs steadily above the wooded slopes overlooking the Manifold. The high limestone bluff of Beeston Tor gradually comes into view along with a fine prospect of the Hamps Valley, Old Park Hill and the village of Grindon across the valley to the northwest.

Eventually the Alstonefield to Grindon road is joined which is followed leftwards for about 800m/875yards to a cattle grid from where a path leads to the left across pastures. From here you can look across the Manifold into the wooded side valley of the Hamps, the main tributary of the Manifold. Rising in a wild, rocky landscape of cotton grass and heather on the eastern flank of Morridge, Hamps means 'summer dry' and during these months the river, just like the Manifold, usually disappears through the faults in the limestone to reappear again near Ilam Hall.

The huge limestone cliff of Beeston Tor, Manifold Valley.

Beyond the pastures the path traverses wooded slopes down to the foot of the spectacular limestone crag of Beeston Tor. In recent years this cliff has become a playground for rock climbers, but it has been known and visited by various cultures over the centuries. In St Bertram's Cave at the foot of the cliff, where the saint is supposed to have lived as a hermit, a cache of Saxon treasures, including coins, rings and brooches, were excavated in the 1920s.

Beeston Tor to Ilam

A series of large stepping-stones are crossed over the usually dry Manifold riverbed to join a track leading up to the left above Beeston Tor Farm. If the river is in spate, then the Grindon road can be followed down to Weag's Bridge where a tarmaced track leads alongside the Manifold to Beeston Tor Farm.

The track continues beyond the farm, past an old barn, to become a path traversing the grassy eastern slopes of Old Park Hill and Mere Hill, climbing steadily through pastureland to the farm buildings at medieval Throwley Hall, whose ruins overlook an old orchard; next door is the Georgian replacement for the original mansion. A narrow hill road linking Ilam and the village of Calton is followed left to a pond below the ruins of Throwley Hall, from where a path leads right across steep grassy slopes and through undulating walled pastures up to Slade House. On this section of the walk you have lovely wide views back up the wooded trench of the Manifold Valley and across to Bunster Hill and Thorpe Cloud.

Beyond Slade House fields lead into the shallow upper dry valley of Musden, just below the hamlet of Calton. Although a dry valley, during periods of heavy rain the path down through the valley can become very muddy. The word Musden means 'mouse infested long sinuous valley', although it is doubtful you will see any mice as you descend through scattered hawthorn scrubland into the long strip of Musden Wood, which in springtime is rich with the scent of wild garlic (ramsons).

At the bottom of the valley, the Musden Grange access track is joined from where a path can be followed southeast through fields down to the footbridge over the Manifold and into the Ilam Country Park. The extensive areas of ridge and furrow cultivation crossed on the way back to Ilam are associated with the former village and provide a charming finish with a fine view of the conical-shaped Bunster Hill, peeping over the woods.

The ruins of Throwley Hall.

Ilam Cross.

INFORMATION

Start/Finish: Ilam (GR 135505). Limited parking in the village; National Trust car park at Ilam Hall.

Distance/Time: 15km(9miles) / 4hours.

Grading: Easy; a walk along hill tracks and paths either side of the lower Manifold valley.

Maps: OS Outdoor Leisure sheet 24 White Peak Area.

Refreshments: The National Trust tea rooms at Ilam Hall.

Public Transport: Limited bus service from Ashbourne and Buxton.

WALK 3 The Manifold Valley and Thor's Cave

South of Hulme End, the sedate River Manifold leaves behind the gritstone and shales and enters the limestone gorge below the massive bulk of Ecton Hill. Here the Manifold Valley, meaning 'many folds' lives up to its name as it twists it way towards Ilam, passing below impressive Thor's cave, etched out of the citadel-like reef limestone crag. Though not quite reaching the grandeur of Dovedale, the section of the Manifold Valley, explored during this walk, is very attractive and provides a 'big-dipper' circular outing.

Our walk starts at the charming village of Wetton, with its grey stone vernacular eighteenth-century farmhouses and barns set around a tiny village green. It also has an interesting parish church of St Margaret, with a fourteenth-century tower. This ancient landscape is littered with various relics of prehistory and even the surrounding narrow, rectangular-shaped fields are part of the long forgotten period before the land enclosures.

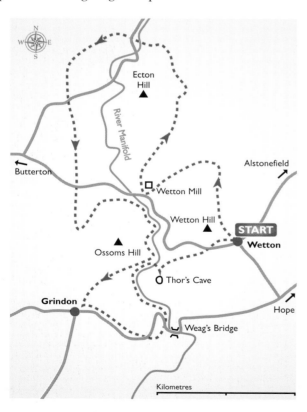

Wetton to Ecton Hill

From the village a lane leads northwest through an old quarried area from where fields are crossed round the flanks of Wetton Hill down to the former Pepper Inn at the head of a dry valley. The inn, built in the eighteenth century, was originally an ale house for miners, and later served as a smallpox isolation hospital and then a button factory.

This steep, open-sided valley leads down around the base of Wetton Hill to arrive in the Manifold Valley at the attractive National Trust buildings of Wetton Mill, once a grist mill but now the site of a popular café on the banks of the river. Above the café is Nan Tor, a rough, pock-marked limestone cave, just one of the many in the valley in which evidence of prehistoric people has been uncovered. The meandering Manifold is a fascinating stretch of water and in dry weather the river disappears just south of Wetton Mill, reappearing again downstream near Ilam Hall.

Just upstream from Wetton Mill, on the eastern side of the river, is Dale Farm where the valley bottom is quitted up a shallow, dry dale past the reef limestone outcrop of Sugar Loaf, and on up past Top of Ecton to near the whaleback summit ridge of Ecton Hill (353m/1158ft). This is one of the highest hills in the area, and is renowned for its fine views, especially northwest to the great east-west watershed at Axe Edge. Ecton Hill is riddled with old mine workings dating back to the seventeenth and eighteenth centuries when Ecton was one of Europe's main producers of copper ore. In its heyday the profits from the mines were considerable and helped the then Duke of Devonshire to pay for Chatsworth House and The Crescent in Buxton.

During the descent of the steep, northern spoil heap slopes to Ecton, you pass two surviving buildings from that enterprising period. However the conspicuous copper-roofed building has no links with the mining days and is a folly built in the 1930s by Arthur Radcliffe.

Thor's Cave.

Wetton Hill seen from the lower slopes of Ossam's Hill.

Ecton to Grindon

Leaving behind the tiny hamlet of Ecton, the valley bottom is crossed and just beyond Dale Bridge, a path climbs the hillside on the left, eventually branching southwest to Villa Farm near Warslow. South of the farm, an amazingly straight path passes through an area of walled fields, isolated farms and woods, crossing several side dales before dropping down into the depths of the valley of the Hoo Brook, a stream that descends from the nearby village of Butterton, eventually becoming a tributary of the Manifold.

A path leads down the Hoo Brook Valley, then via Water Slacks below the dense woods of the National Trust's Ossam's Hill, and along the curving valley to reach the valley floor again near Wetton Mill. The valley road leads southwards over Dafar Bridge to join the tarmaced

track along the winding route of the old railway – keep an eye open for cyclists on this popular trail. Eventually you arrive below the wooded slopes overlooked by the spectacular Thor's Cave, the main attraction in this section of the valley.

A visit to the cave is for later, though. Instead, our way leads steeply right up through Ladyside Wood, eventually crossing pastureland to Grindon. During the climb to the village you get great views back across to Thor's Cave. Grindon, whose name means 'green hill', is dominated by its parish church, often referred to as 'the Cathedral of Staffordshire Moorlands', whose octagonal spire is a landmark for miles. The seventeenth-century Cavalier Inn makes a pleasant break in the walk.

Grindon to Wetton

In the valley bottom to the east of the village lies Weag's Bridge, approached from Grindon along a narrow hill road. At a very sharp bend a path descends steeply through fields to Weag's Bridge. No cars are allowed north of the bridge through this section of the valley which gives a pleasant stroll along the meandering tarmaced track. At one bend in the track you are greeted by a dramatic view of Thor's Cave in the huge limestone cliff towering over the narrow confines of the wooded valley.

Cross the river by a footbridge and climb a stepped path steeply up the wooded slopes to the cave with its gently rising floor. Care is needed on the sloping, polished limestone rocks at the entrance to the cave, but once inside the huge dome you feel dwarfed by its scale. Light also

Thor's Cave from above Ladyside Wood.

The summit of Thor's Cave and the upper reaches of the Manifold Valley.

enters the cave from another opening, the West Window, but the prospect outwards through the massive main entrance is one of the highlights of the walk. The cave was crudely excavated by Victorian enthusiasts and the various artefacts found indicated signs of very early occupation by Upper Paleolithic hunting bands, probably using the Manifold Valley as a summer camp.

An easy way leads up the hillside round the left side of the cave to the lofty summit of the crag from where you can look across to Ossam's Hill and northwards up the twisting Manifold Valley to the Wetton and Ecton Hills. A concessionary path now leads back through fields and a walled lane to Wetton village.

INFORMATION
Start/Finish: Car park at Wetton village (GR 109553).
Distance/Time: 17km(10miles) / 5hours.
Grading: Moderate; mainly on good footpaths but some steep climbs involved.
Maps: OS Outdoor Leisure sheet 24 White Peak Area.
Refreshments: Royal Oak at Wetton and the Cavalier Inn at Grindon; café at Wetton Mill.
Public Transport: Bus service from Ashbourne.

Hartington and Pilsbury Castle

Between Hartington and Crowdecote is a quiet, unspoilt area of gentle rolling countryside in which a young, impatient River Dove prepares itself for the turbulent journey through the more rugged dales to the south. For walkers looking for a quiet half-day walk away from the more popular dales, this broader and more open section of the Upper Dove Valley provides a pleasant outing exploring the valley and its eastern limestone flanks beyond Hartington, returning through grit-stone pastureland on its western rim. During the walk you also visit Pilsbury Castle one of the most interesting medieval sites in the Peak.

The bustling limestone village of Hartington is the 'capital' of the Upper Dove Valley. With its church and fine old buildings including Hartington Hall, a superb early-seventeenth-century Jacobean-style building (now a youth hostel), pubs, hotels, cafés, cheese factory and shops, the village is very popular at weekends and Bank Holidays and has become something of a 'honeypot'.

Hartington to Pilsbury castle

From the village pond, or 'mere', the way is northwards along Dig Street and just after the drive entrance to Moat Hall a walled green lane climbs rightwards to join Hide Lane. A short distance along the lane, a path leads left across fields on the flanks of Carder Low. On this section you have expansive views up the Dove valley to the shapely reef limestone peaks near Longnor. Eventually the path drops down to join a side valley, part of an old saltway route from Cheshire to Chesterfield that crossed the northern slopes of Sheen Hill (380m/1247ft), visible beyond the farming hamlet of Pilsbury on the opposite side of the Dove in Staffordshire.

After heading left along the minor valley, past a mere and limestone marker post, a narrow hill road dipping steeply to Pilsbury, is crossed to join a series of walled fields leading down to the enigmatic Pilsbury Castle, overlooked by a crag of reef limestone. This large earthwork has all the features of a Norman motte and bailey castle and it seems that the fortification was built around 1100. The general consensus is that it was probably built over the site of a much older fort, possibly Iron Age, and might have been the focal point of an early settlement for the Upper Dove.

Crowdecote to Hartington

Continuing beyond the earthworks, the eastern bank of the river is followed up the valley towards Bridge End Farm and Crowdecote (in Old English 'Cruda's cottage'), with its Pack Horse Inn and cottages tumbled together on a hillside from where the unique reef limestone hills of the Upper Dove are seen. The return journey from Crowdecote lies south-east from near Bridge End Farm across a footbridge over the Dove into Staffordshire. A footpath traverses steeply through fields, passing close to the farms at Upper Whittle and Under Whittle, to join the minor road below the mock castle of Sheen Hill. After the pastoral limestone scenery on the Derbyshire flanks of the Dove the Staffordshire side is in marked contrast consisting of bleak, high gritstone moorland farms with pastureland criss-crossed by miles of drystone walls.

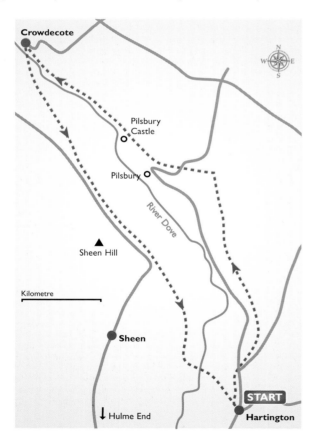

Approaching Pilsbury Castle.

Left: *Sheen Hill rises beyond Pilsbury Castle.*

Below: *Hartington Hall, now a youth hostel.*

The narrow hill road traverses the flanks of Sheen Hill along the rim of the valley towards the upland village of Sheen. At a sharp bend by Harris Close Farm, a footpath leads alongside an unusual banktop wall through a series of fields. To your right is Sheen, with its conspicuous Victorian church and its pyramid-topped tower visible through the trees. Beyond the fields the path crosses the top of a steep scar slope then meanders along the upper edge of a small conifer plantation before making a steep diagonal descent through gorse and hawthorn scrub. From the hillside path you get a great view over Hartington.

Our way back to Hartington is over meadows down to the Dove and so back into Derbyshire, where fields are crossed to arrive at the forecourt of the Dairy Crest cheese factory on the edge of the village. As you amble left into the village, past the cheese shop, why not sample some Hartington Stilton, one of the local specialties?

Storm over High Wheeldon, near Crowdecote.

WALK 5 The Reef Hills of the Upper Dove

South of the moorland escarpment of Axe Edge is a green, folded landscape, dotted with farms, crossed by old packhorse routes and backed by a range of sharply-etched hills, which under their winter mantle of snow look like a distant scene from the Alps. These hills include High Wheeldon (422m/1383ft), Parkhouse Hill (372m/1221ft) and Chrome Hill (430m/1411ft) which are the remnants of coral reefs which surrounded a shallow sea about 350 million years ago. Keep an eye open for fossils of crinoids (sea lilies), brachiopods and corals in the drystone walls.

The two shapeliest of these miniature gems are Chrome and Parkhouse Hills and when seen in profile their undulating crests look like a child's drawing of a dragon's back (which is indeed the local name for them). Despite the name Peak District, real peaks are a rarity in the National Park, but the Upper Dove Valley certainly appears to have more than its fair share.

Starting from the village of Earl Sterndale, a fascinating circular route with geological and archaeological associations can be followed through this remarkable landscape. The walk criss-crosses limestone dales and ridges, ascends sharp peaks, visits the upland villages of Longnor and Hollinsclough, and takes in many interesting features.

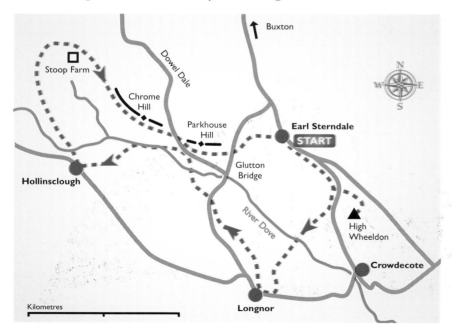

Chrome Hill and Parkhouse Hill seen from Hitter Hill near Earl Sterndale.

High Wheeldon.

Below: *Crossing the 'Dragon's Back'. Axe Edge in the distance.*

Looking from High Wheeldon to Longnor. Evening sunshine highlights the ancient ridge-and-furrow cultivation strips.

Earl Sterndale to Longnor

The limestone cottages of Earl Sterndale nestle around the small village green, and opposite the church of St Michael is the local inn with the unusual name of The Quiet Woman Inn. The sign board inscription reads 'Soft words turneth away wrath' and depicts a headless woman, apparently the treatment offered by a former landlord to his nagging wife known as 'Chattering Charteris'. From the inn a narrow road is followed southeasterly past the village pond down to Aldery Cliff.

Opposite the cliff, and approached by steep grassy slopes from a National Trust roadside stile, is the conical-shaped peak of High Wheeldon. Apart from serving as a war memorial, the small summit provides one of the finest accessible viewpoints in the Upper Dove Valley, and from here you get a lovely perspective of the hills and across to Longnor and the Manifold Valley. Just below the summit is the gated Fox Hole Cave, one of the many sites in the area where archaeological remains dating back to Neolithic and Palaeolithic times have been found.

Down the road from Aldery Cliff, a green lane can be followed right down to Beggar's Bridge spanning the Dove, from where a footpath crosses an area of ancient ridge-and-furrow cultivation before climbing up to Top o'th'Edge and a walled lane leading into Longnor. The village, with its cobbled market place and dark houses, stands at an old turnpike cross-roads and is also on the boundary between the Staffordshire gritstone moors and limestone country. Longnor was once a market centre for the region and has a Victorian market hall built in 1873. Now a craft centre and café, the hall retains a fascinating inscription over the entrance showing the tariffs of bygone market tolls.

Top: *Parkhouse Hill.*

Above: *Chrome Hill and Parkhouse Hill.*

Right: *A crossing of the 'Dragon's Back' is an exciting prospect when the hill is covered in snow.*

Longnor to Hollinsclough

From the Market Square the way lies north up narrow Chapel Street to eventually follow a lane between ruined farm buildings from where a footpath crosses fields to join a farm track leading to Yew Tree Grange and along to the B5053 Buxton road. The road is followed right and just before it dips towards Glutton Bridge, a lane branches left to Dove Bank and a wooden footbridge over the infant Dove to join the narrow lane below Parkhouse Hill.

Along this section of the walk the tiny, yet rugged hills of Chrome and Parkhouse, with their saw-toothed summit ridges have become steadily more impressive. Now they rear up majestically from the flat, green valley floor at the entrance to Dowel Dale, which separates the two hills. Chrome Hill derives its name from the Old English word 'crum' meaning 'sickle-shaped' which aptly describes its curved serrated ridge, while Parkhouse Hill's name has historical connections with the former monastic Glutton Grange.

Our route now heads sharp left along the banks of the River Dove via Hollins Farm track, which soon branches left to join a minor road leading to the settlement of Hollinsclough, with its cottages and farmhouse set around a crossroads. The hamlet once had a silk weaving cottage industry, supplying mills in Macclesfield during the eighteenth century.

Hollinsclough to Earl Sterndale

Just north of the cluster of houses, a track leads down to a packhorse bridge, a lovely spot in spring with the scent of white blossom of hawthorn and rowan in the air. This whole area is criss-crossed by old packhorse ways, and jaggers (the packhorse leaders) probably brought their lines of packhorses this way from Flash or Leek on their way to Buxton and beyond.

From the bridge our way lies up tracks on the western flanks of Hollins Hill then round to Stoop Farm and the start of the most spectacular part of the walk, a traverse of Chrome Hill. A concessionary path near the farm takes you over the narrow, saw-toothed ridge which drops and rises in a series of small grass and rocky arêtes. The steep drops all around give a real feeling of space and make the hill appear much bigger than its modest height suggests. The ascent is one of the best ridge scrambles in the White Peak, albeit an easy one and under a mantle of snow the crossing of the ridge can be quite exciting.

From the ridge you can really appreciate the views, especially west to the rolling gritstone moors of Staffordshire's Oliver Hill and Axe Edge which fill the skyline. However, it is the end-on view of Parkhouse Hill, with its steep grass and rocky arete sweeping up above the limestone buttress known as the Sugar Loaf, that manages to surprise walkers.

The steep southern grassy ridge is followed easily down to the narrow road that runs through Dowel Dale. Made of softer rocks this narrow, inter-coral reef channel worn down by water drainage over aeons of time has been inhabited by numerous groups as far back as nomadic hunters, maybe 10,000 years ago, and right up to modern times, where sheep farming now dominates the dale. At the bottom of the dry dale, opposite Dowall Hall, is Dowel Cave, which has revealed evidence of Palaeolithic occupation.

An ascent of Parkhouse Hill looks very attractive, but unfortunately it is on private land and at present there is no access agreement for a direct ascent. However, a path does traverse its southern flanks to join the road near Glutton Bridge from where a path climbs up to the brow of Hitter Hill. This is a great viewpoint, especially in winter or late evening when the reef hills are seen at their best, more so if you manage to be there for a fine sunset. All that now remains is a short walk across a couple of fields back to Earl Sterndale.

INFORMATION
Start/Finish: Earl Sterndale GR 090670.
Distance/Time: 14km(9miles) / 5hours.
Grading: Moderate; a walk along footpaths, tracks and narrow hill roads but with several steep ascents and some airy ridge scrambling.
Maps: OS Outdoor Leisure sheet 24 White Peak Area.
Refreshments: The Quiet Woman at Earl Sterndale, cafés and pubs at Longnor and the Pack Horse Inn at Crowdecote.
Public Transport: Buses from Buxton and Hartington.

THE WESTERN PEAK

Some of the most beautiful and romantic countryside of the Peak District is found outside Derbyshire to the west, in Staffordshire and Cheshire. What could be more charming than the deep, wooded valley of the Dane near Bosley Minn and Wincle Minn, or more mysterious than the shadowed green of Macclesfield Forest and the Dale of Goyt?

To the north, near Disley, is Lyme Hall with its extensive wooded park, where, if you walk up through the trees to the open moor, the whole of western Peakland is revealed. A tilted upland of narrow ridges, pointed summits and green dales criss-crossed by narrow hill roads and medieval packhorse routes are a foreground for the broad sweep of the Cheshire Plain. Indeed, one of the remarkable features of this western part of the region is the manner in which the wild, high moors sweep down suddenly to give way to fertile lowland. It is also a landscape once notorious for highwaymen and coin forgers.

Shutlingsloe is the outstanding hill shape of the area, dominating the village of Wildboarclough. The neighbouring Dane Valley winds down from open moors to heavily wooded dales dotted with farms and the mysterious Lud's Church. It is altogether a delightful, unassuming corner of England.

The Goyt Valley, with its two reservoirs, has forgotten farms, ruined Errwood Hall and the remains of the Cromford and High Peak Railway slanting across its eastern slopes; and maturing, coniferous plantations range towards its breezy western watershed, another exceptional viewpoint.

All this is fine walking country, as good as any in the district and with its own particular magic, counterpoints of hill pastures, open moor, woodland and parkland fringing the limestone and gritstone heart of the Peak District.

The Roaches.

Shutlingsloe is the dominant feature in the Western Peak.

WALK 6 The Roaches and Three Shire Heads

Between Buxton, Macclesfield and Leek is an area of well-defined craggy ridges, rolling moorland and wooded valleys cut by narrow lanes and old packhorse routes, including parts of Derbyshire, Cheshire and Staffordshire. Starting from the Cat and Fiddle Inn, the second highest pub in England, this wild and rugged landscape can be explored by this long circular walk. High moors lead south to Three Shire Heads, where the three counties rub shoulders at an old packhorse bridge, then the Roaches escarpment is traversed before returning via Flash and the great watershed of Axe Edge Moor.

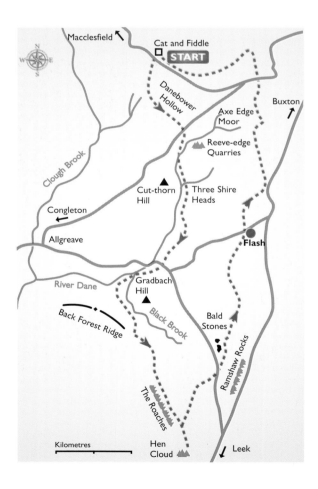

Cat and Fiddle Inn to Three Shire Heads

Starting from the A537 Buxton to Macclesfield Road at the Cat and Fiddle Inn, set in a moorland wilderness, a bridleway crosses open moorland to Danebower Hollow, and the A54 Buxton-Congleton Road. Beyond the road a path drops down heather-covered slopes past a chimney and a few crumbling buildings, relics of the days when stone was extracted from Reeves Edge on the hillside opposite.

Here, on the moors of Axe Edge, the infant River Dane rises and can be followed along its Cheshire side to the packhorse bridge at Three Shire Heads. Tucked in a hollow, surrounded by bracken and heather-clad slopes, this is a seductive place to pause and explore the cascades of water which tumble into Pannier's Pool, named after the bags which were slung on each side of the packhorses. Highwaymen, coiners and law breakers once used this border land as an escape route into the neighbouring county to avoid arrest, and its secluded nature made it a popular venue for cock fighting and many a bare-knuckle prize fight also took place here.

Above: *The Roaches.*

Left: *The Cat and Fiddle pub sign.*

Three Shire Heads to the Roaches

Beyond the deep, brown pool an old packhorse way is followed across the southern flanks of Tor Edge, to join a path down a broad ridge through fields, to Manor Farm where a narrow road beside the River Dane leads to Gradbach Mill. Built in 1875 and originally used for flax and silk spinning and later carpet making, the stone mill building is now a youth hostel. A pleasant riverside stroll downstream brings us to a footbridge at the confluence with Black Brook, below the steep slopes of Forest Wood. Beyond the bridge, paths lead left up through a mixture of oak, larch and pine to the narrow hill road at Roach End where fine views are obtained back across the Dane Valley to Shutlingsloe. Further west are Bosley Cloud and Mow Cop, backed by views across the Cheshire Plain to Wales.

From Roach End a constructed path weaves its way through an area of wind-sculptured rocks up to a trig point and the start of one of the most spectacular sections of the walk along the craggy spine of the Roaches escarpment. The crest of the almost unbroken rocks stretches for more than 2km/1.25miles to the pointed summit of Hen Cloud. Rough, brown buttresses rear up above decaying woodland and dominate the surrounding moors. Just beyond a peaty hollow containing Doxey Pool, mentioned in the Domesday Book and where legend has it that the ghost of a young singing mermaid attracts young men to a watery end, the rocks reach their highest point. Here, two impressive tiers have formed to provide some of the best gritstone climbing in the Peak District.

Built into the lower tier and approached down a stone staircase, is Rockhall, a quaint Grimm's fairy-tale cottage, a place with a chequered history from the early gamekeeping days, when this area was private land. It is now a climbers' bunkhouse.

Beyond the cottage across a grassy nick, sits the imposing rocky sentinel of Hen Cloud with its castle-like buttresses set above a steep, fern-covered hillside overlooking the tiny hamlet of Upper Hulme. Few other Peakland outcrops can challenge this impressive sentinel for its mountain-like setting. Despite having to retrace your steps, the short, steep climb to the top is well worth the effort for the views northwards of the twisted crenellated ridge of Ramshaw Rocks, and beyond, the boggy acres of Goldsitch Moss stretching away towards Axe Edge.

The packhorse bridge at Three Shire Heads.

Right: *The dramatic rock architecture of the Roaches' lower tier.*

Hen Cloud to the Cat and Fiddle

From the grassy col between Hen Cloud and the Roaches, tracks are followed north to join a narrow hill leading right to a cottage, and the start of Newstones ridge. This is followed past many eroded boulders and pinnacles, finally traversing round a hillside through a conifer plantation to Gib Tor Farm. Beyond the farm, paths cross rough sheep farming country to Flash Bottom near a dog-leg bend in the quiet lane leading up to the village of Flash.

Situated at 463m/1518ft, and supposedly the highest village in England, Flash is a cluster of weatherworn cottages huddled together at the foot of Oliver Hill, the highest point in Staffordshire. It was the haunt of rogues and coin forgers who became known as 'Flash men'. The village name became infamous through its association with 'Flash money', forged currency which circulated throughout England. In fact anything that was not quite as good as it looked was referred to as 'flashy' – a term still used today.

Above left: *A misty morning at the Roaches.*

Above right: *Doxey Pool.*

North of Flash, a path leads over the flanks of Oliver Hill to join a narrow lane to Axe Edge End from where footpaths can be followed to Dane Head, a wild place in the middle of Axe Edge Moor, where the trilling of larks and the wildness of bog, bilberry and heather tufts greet the walker. The old fenced and capped mine shafts dotted about are a reminder of a bygone age when a modest yield of coal, mainly for local domestic use, was dug out of thin seams here.

This high moorland is also renowned for the number of famous rivers it spawns including the Dove, Manifold, Wye, Dane and Goyt; and also for its extensive views. To the east are the sharp-edged and miniature reef-limestone peaks of the Upper Dove Valley, backed by the gentle country of the White Peak, fading into the distance. This view is in marked contrast with the nearby view over Buxton to Combs Moss with the dark, brooding mass of Kinder Scout beyond.

A good path continues across the moor to the A54 and beyond to the track of the old turnpike road, which descends gently leftwards into the upper reaches of the Goyt Valley, from where a narrow hill road climbs back to the Cat and Fiddle.

The Newstones ridge.

Crossing Axe Edge moors.

Sunset over Tittesworth Reservoir.

49

WALK 7   Lud's Church and the Dane Valley

Between Dane Head, high on Axe Edge Moor, and the village of Wincle, the young River Dane and its converging tiny streams rush through a landscape of rumpled gritstone hills. It dips under the packhorse bridge at Three Shire Heads, before breaking out along the narrow wooded Dane Valley downstream from Gradbach, to continue on its way westwards across the Cheshire Plain. Although much of the Dane may be followed from its source along a series of riverbank footpaths, this would miss out much of the surrounding moorland uplands.

A more varied and interesting walk, and a more demanding one, is to start from the village of Wincle which nestles in a dell above the Dane and follows a series of paths and old packhorse routes, crossing and recrossing the river course. The walk also seeks out the enigmatic Lud's Church, hidden in the wooded slopes below the craggy ridge of Back Forest, finally returning to Wincle via the leafy lanes and hillsides around Wildboarclough and Allgreave.

Wincle to Lud's Church

Starting from just east of Wincle's St Michael's parish church and village school near Hammerton Farm, a path descends a field and crosses the stream in wooded Hog Clough. After traversing above the top edge of a wood, a farm lane is crossed from where you can look left and see the tilted crag of the Hanging Stone on the distant skyline, visited later. The path now descends steeply through fields to the high, single-arched bridge that crosses the slow moving Dane and gives its name to the hamlet of Danebridge, with its cluster of gritstone houses hidden among trees.

First mentioned in 1357 before the bridge was built, this crossing was known as Slider Ford – so named because of its slippery banks – and was part of a medieval highway connecting Leek with Macclesfield. Just west of here, and backed by the whaleback of Minn Hill, is the remote, former monastic Wincle Grange, certainly one of the oldest farmhouses in the southern Pennines.

After crossing the road bridge from Cheshire into Staffordshire, a track descends through woodland to a riverside path which soon quits the meadows and climbs through oak and birch woodland high above the river to emerge on the open grassland of Back Dane. A waymarked path passes several houses to their right, before descending again to re-enter more woodland overlooking the Dane that gently flows below gritstone crags through a wooded gorge.

The path follows an undulating course through the trees, finally arriving at a footbridge at the confluence with Black Brook below the steep slopes of Forest Wood. From the footbridge, a path signposted for Swythamley Hall climbs through a mixture of oak, larch and pine up to the fort-like outcrop of gritstone rocks known as Castle Cliff. Along a footpath to the left lies the hidden Lud's Church, a narrow, tree-veiled chasm between mossy walls, with steps carved out of the rocky floor. To Victorians, it was one of the 'Wonders of the Peak' and like the place itself, the name of Lud's Church is quite intriguing. Possibly associated with Walter de Ludauk, a follower of Wycliff in the fourteenth century who may have held services here; it has also been linked with the Luddites and could well have provided the setting for the Green Chapel sought by Sir Gawain in the early medieval poem, *Sir Gawain and the Green Knight*. Whatever it was used for, this natural cleft in the hillside is a fascinating place to explore and the dank, fern-coated gorge exudes atmosphere.

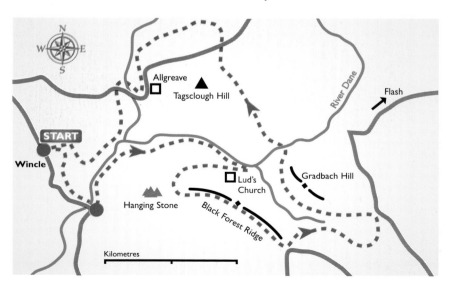

Crossing the Back Forest ridge.

Traversing the flanks of Gradbach Hill towards Gradbach.

Looking northwest from Roach End across Gradbach to Shutlingsloe.

Lud's Church to Gradbach

Back at Castle Cliff Rocks the path continues up to the western end of Back Forest ridge a short distance from the bold crag known as the Hanging Stone which can be reached by a short detour across fields. Steps lead down the side of the rock where you can see a plaque set into the rock which commemorates 'Burke, a noble black mastiff, a gun and a ramble his heart's desire, with the friend of his life, the Swythamley squire. 1874'. Swythamley Hall lies hidden by trees just to the south.

A concessionary path now holds the crest of the ridge from where you can take in the fine views back across the Dane Valley to the cone-shaped peak of Shutlingsloe, while further west are Bosley Cloud and Mow Cop, backed by the Cheshire Plain. Sweeping south from here is the Roaches ridge, with its impressive gritstone outcrops rearing up above heather and tree-clad slopes.

At the narrow hill road at Roach End, first a lane, then a path descends left past a farmhouse down to Black Brook and the mossy hollow of Goldsitch Moss, with its boggy pools and old mine shafts where coal was hacked out from thin seams long ago. Here are to be found the handsome bog asphodel, sphagnum moss and nearby, a rich growth of cranberry occurs, reputedly the most luxuriant in the Peak District. This quiet, peaceful place is also the haunt of herons and waders.

Footpaths climb out of the valley to join a track leading left across walled fields on the western flanks of Gradbach Hill. The track leads to the Scout campsite at Gradbach, just below which, on the edge of the River Dane, stands the renovated Gradbach Mill, now a popular youth hostel. Several old packhorse routes pass this way; one follows the river northwards to Three Shire Heads, the other, which we take, links Gradbach Mill with Wildboarclough.

Gradbach to Wilboarclough

Beyond the modern footbridge over the Dane, the steep, typical narrow packhorse way climbs up to the Allgreave road, yet another old way, and the eighteenth-century house, The Eagle and Child. This was originally an inn where the jaggers leading their packhorse trains would slake their thirst while the horses drank from the nearby stone water troughs. The track continues across Tagsclough Hill, from where Shutlingsloe dominates the scene ahead, then crosses the A54 Buxton-Congleton road to pass Berrybank Wood, and finally descends to the village lanes of Wildboarclough.

The damp ravine of Lud's Church.

Looking from Back Forest ridge towards the Roaches.

Our way now lies south along the valley road past the Crag Inn for about about 500m/550yards to the Brookside Restaurant where a footbridge crosses Clough Brook. From here a path meanders along the riverbank, finally crossing meadows below a wood to join a track climbing up to the Rose and Crown pub at Allgreave. Just below the pub, tucked into the hairpin bend, is a tiny Methodist church that is passed down to the road junction leading leftwards to Wincle.

At Allmeadows Farm a good path leads into the valley and traverses above the wooded slopes overlooking the Dane. The final section of the walk back to Wincle is along a farm track round the western flanks of Hill Top, with a last glimpse across Danebridge to the wooded parklands of Swythamley Hall.

INFORMATION
Start/Finish: Wincle GR 961661.
Distance/Time: 21km(13miles) / 6hours.
Grading: Easy; along moorland paths, old packhorse routes and riverside paths through a beautiful, wooded valley.
Maps: OS Outdoor Leisure 24 White Peak Area.
Refreshments: The Ship Inn, Wincle; the Crag Inn, Wildboarclough; Rose and Crown, Allgreave.
Public Transport: Railway station at Buxton for bus service to Congleton.

WALK 8 Shutlingsloe and Macclesfield Forest

For great views across the deeply cut-valleys and ridges of the western fringes of the Peak District, a walk over shapely Shutlingsloe takes some beating. The peak dominates the area and looks down over Macclesfield Forest. In Norman times this royal hunting forest stretched for 24km/15miles from Marple in the north to Bosley in the south. Now all that remains from before legal disafforestation and enclosure of this vast tract of royal forest in the seventeenth century, is the lonely Forest Chapel hamlet at an altitude of 365m/1198ft.

This pleasant and varied circular walk through eastern Cheshire involves steep ascents to the splendid viewpoints at Shutlingsloe and Tegg's Nose, linked by forest paths, open moorland and rural byways. A good starting point is the Tegg's Nose Country Park, based on an old gritstone quarry on the Buxton to Macclesfield Old Road.

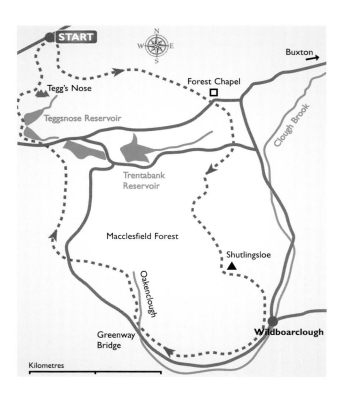

Tegg's Nose to Shutlingsloe

From the car park at Tegg's Nose, a concessionary walled bridleway signposted Saddlers Way (an ancient packhorse route), descends steep slopes to a lane. The lane leads right past Clough House then up to another farmhouse, bypassed on its left by a stony path. Eventually the path becomes very narrow and rocky as it climbs steeply between walls to join Hacked Lane Way at Hardingland, just beyond which Macclesfield Forest is entered.

An excellent path traverses conifer-clad slopes to join a bridleway leading right down to a narrow hill road and Macclesfield Forest Chapel hamlet overlooked by Toot Hill. This isolated hamlet is a cluster of former farms and its parish church of St Stephen is where a traditional rushbearing ceremony is held each August. Rushes taken from the nearby moor are spread over the floor of the decorated church – a practice dating back to when this was a commonly used form of floor covering.

After a visit to this fascinating chapel, take the narrow hill road opposite which drops southeast, before swinging right up to a T-junction, where you re-enter Macclesfield Forest. A stony track descends past the derelict Ferriser Farm then climbs gently through woodland to a stile at the moor edge.

Once the forest is left, a re-constructed path crosses High Moor to where a gritstone staircase leads steeply up to the summit of Shutlingsloe (506m/1660ft). This is one of the shapeliest of conical hills in the area, and on clear days you can appreciate splendid panoramic views embracing the dark profiles of the Staffordshire moorlands and the Whetstone Ridge backed by Axe Edge. Across to the west, the Welsh hills and Merseyside are often visible, while to the north the rolling hills of the conifered Macclesfield Forest tilt towards the Cheshire Plain where, on a clear day, Jodrell Bank radio telescope can be seen.

Shutlingsloe overlooking Wildboarclough.

The view southwest from Tegg's Nose across Macclesfield Forest to Shutlingsloe.

Shutlingsloe to Bottoms Reservoir

A waymarker on the summit rocks points the way down steep slopes to Wildboarclough, whose open hill pastures and hill farms clinging to small terraces make this one of the most attractive parts of the National Park. After an initial rocky section, the path eases to more gentle grassy slopes down to a farm access lane curving rightwards above woodland down to a road.

Wildboarclough, a wooded valley of scattered farms and cottages, lies to the left over the bridge but our way is right to the Crag Inn. Just beyond the inn car park a grassy path contours between hawthorn and gorse bushes across the lower slopes of Mount Pleasant, eventually bearing right above Lower Nabbs Farm to a walled lane leading left down to the valley road near Greenway Bridge.

From the bridge the banks of the stream can be followed up Oaken Clough passing two ponds to join the drive to Oakenclough Farm at the edge of High Moor. A grassy path crosses the broad moor, past some pools, and then drops down between walls to emerge onto the road at the Hanging Gate public house. Beyond the pub's yard, a path slants rightwards down grassy fields to a narrow road and the Gritstone Trail, a long walk linking Lyme Park in the north with Rushton Spencer.

Paths, waymarked with the Gritstone Trail's yellow boot-print, cross through walled farmland to join a road alongside Bottoms Reservoir, one of a chain of four reservoirs which include the secluded Ridgegate and Trentabank Reservoirs surrounded by tall conifers just to the east in Macclesfield Forest. The reservoirs provide excellent bird sanctuaries, particular as a stopover for winter migrants, and are great places for birdwatchers.

Bottoms Reservoir to Tegg's Nose

The conspicuous quarry-worked ridge-top dominating the slopes ahead is Tegg's Nose, our next objective, approached across the two dam walls of Bottoms and Tegg's Nose Reservoirs just down the road to the left. After crossing the dam walls, a steep path climbs through the oak and mountain ash of Teggsnose Wood then up the grassy slopes of Ward's Knob into the country park, with its excellent views over Langley and the Cheshire Plain. Beside the quarry is a display of old machinery dating back to the time when much of the good building stone used for local farms and cottages was extracted.

The quarry was at its most productive in the late 1800s and quarrying eventually came to an end here in 1955. From the quarry promenade, where nature is now regaining a foothold with trees and heather, you can look westwards and pick out the curving Macclesfield Canal beyond the buttery gorse banks on nearby Ward's Knob and Blakelow Hill. As ever, the familiar shape of Shutlingsloe is visible rearing above the southeastern horizon.

From the quarry a stony track leads back to the car park and the end of the walk.

Clockwise, from top left:
Approaching the summit of Shutlingsloe.

Shutlingsloe seen from near the Cat and Fiddle Inn.

Forest Chapel.

Shining Tor seen from near Forest Chapel.

INFORMATION
Start/Finish: Car park at Tegg's Nose Country Park GR 950732.
Distance/Time: 17km(10.5miles) / 5–6hours.
Grading: Moderate; along good woodland tracks, field and moorland foot-paths with some steep ascents and descents.
Maps: OS Outdoor Leisure 24 The White Peak.
Refreshments: Crag Inn and Hanging Gate Inn; Tegg's Nose Information Centre.
Public Transport: Railway stations at Macclesfield and Buxton, linked by bus route close to Tegg's Nose.

WALK 9 Shining Tor and the Goyt Valley

The River Goyt starts its long journey on the bleak gritstone moors of Axe Edge and Goyt Moss before flowing through the Goyt Valley northwards to become the Mersey. The upper part of the Goyt Valley, set within one of the folds of hill country west of Buxton, contains a Roman road and packhorse route and was briefly affected by industry when the Cromford and High Peak Railway cut through its eastern flanks and even gritstone quarries and coal mines made a fleeting appearance.

Despite the valley's two reservoirs with their attendant car parks and picnic areas and afforestation, the valley still retains much of its wildness. By following the high moors along the valley rim, including an ascent of Shining Tor together with the interesting sections around the reservoirs, a diverse and fascinating circular outing can be had starting from Buxton.

The old spa town of Buxton nestles in a sheltered hollow between the dark, gritstone moors of the western Peak District and the rolling limestone hills and dales of the White Peak. The Romans were attracted here by the warm springs that emerge near the River Wye and they built baths and brought roads from their military stations to their settlement of *Aquae Arnemetiae*. In the following centuries these springs became a place of pilgrimage for invalids seeking the cure. Even Mary Queen of Scots came here to drink and bathe in the waters to seek relief from her rheumatism.

The town has some fine buildings dating from its heyday as a fashionable spa including the magnificent Crescent, built by the Duke of Devonshire in the 1780s opposite the warm spring at St Ann's Well. Other fine buildings include the recently-closed Devonshire Royal Hospital, with its huge dome – at one time the largest in the world – the superb Pavilion Gardens and the Opera House.

Buxton to Errwood

Starting from Burbage Church on the western outskirts of Buxton, Bishop's Lane is followed beside the Cavendish Golf Course to a path climbing steeply up to open moorland where the full sweep of the Goyt Valley opens up. After descending grassy slopes you arrive at a blocked-off tunnel and dismantled railway track. Completed in 1826, Cromford and High Peak line crossed central Peakland linking the canal at Cromford with the Peak Forest Canal at Whaley Bridge. The embankment, which carried the line, can be seen sweeping around the head of Wildmoorstone Clough above Errwood Reservoir. Operating from 1831 to about 1894, this stretch of the track leads to the Bunsal Incline, a 1 in 7 gradient where a steam engine was needed to haul up loaded goods wagons.

Beyond the tunnel entrance the walk continues down the grass and heather slopes of the picturesque clough through which Wildmoorstone Brook wends its quiet way. At the bottom of the clough, first a track and then footpath lead right across wooded slopes round Bunsal Cob overlooking Errwood Reservoir.

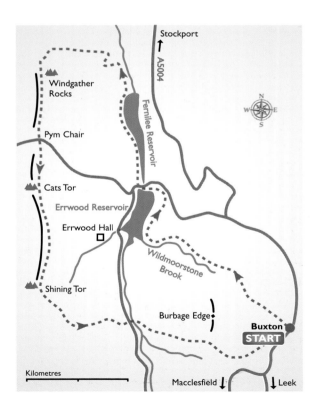

The view north across Goyt Forest from near Pym Chair.

59

Berry Clough, Goyt Valley.

Errwood Reservoir.

The ruins of Errwood Hall, Goyt Valley.

A difficult winter crossing of Burbage Edge.

Prior to flooding, the valley contained a thriving community near Goyt's Bridge, and later a packhorse crossing. The bridge was eventually dismantled and moved further upstream near an old gritstone quarry, originally worked by Thomas Pickford whose packhorses were the forerunners of the famous Pickford's Removal Company. The Grimshawes, a wealthy family who lived in nearby Errwood Hall, dominated this part of the Goyt Valley in the nineteenth century. However, as a result of Stockport's ever-increasing demand for water, Fernilee Reservoir was built and thirty years later a second reservoir, Errwood, was built higher up the valley.

In 1938 the house was partly demolished and sadly the only remains of this once fine hall are a few crumbled walls amid rhododendrons and azaleas, in the woods on the southwestern side of the reservoir. The Grimshawes planted over 40,000 azaleas and rhododendrons and their legacy is a landscape aglow with colour in the early summer. The ruins are worth seeking out, as is the small circular Spanish Shrine, built by the Grimshawes in memory of their governess, Dolores de Bergin. The shrine, sheltered by pine trees, lies up a small side valley beyond the ruins.

Looking south from the summit of Shining Tor towards Shutlingsloe.

Errwood to Shining Tor

From the road that crosses Errwood's dam wall you can look down on Fernilee Reservoir along whose left shore, overlooked by the densely-wooded slopes of Hoo Moor, the walk continues. This quiet section along paths and tracks through mixed woodland leads pleasantly to Fernilee's dam wall, from where a lane can be followed, eventually climbing past Overton Hall Farm. Just beyond the farm a path climbs up grassy slopes and joins the wooded crest of the moorland ridge near the popular and aptly named Windgather Rocks, a great place for introducing beginners to rock climbing.

From the crag, the broad heathery ridge separating the Todd and Goyt valleys is followed up to Pym Chair where the Roman Road known as The Street crosses the ridge. It was just beyond here, at the col known as Old Gate Nick, that salt-trading jaggers used to cross the ridge after climbing up out of the Todd Valley above Saltersford Hall, along their trade route from Cheshire to Chesterfield and beyond.

The next part of the walk now lies ahead between Cats Tor and Shining Tor along the crest of a ridge that separates Cheshire from Derbyshire. An alternative way is to follow tracks along the lower western flanks of these tops through a patchwork of pastureland that's changed little in the last few centuries, eventually rejoining the ridge near the summit of Shining Tor. That way the pretty Jenkin Chapel, looking more like a house with a defensive tower at one end than a rural church, can be visited.

The once boggy track beside the dry-stone wall that clings to the crest of the ridge has been improved in recent years and the going is now much easier, allowing you to enjoy the surrounding views as you amble up towards the summit of Shining Tor (559m/1834ft). On a clear day you have expansive views north to Sponds Hill, Chinley Churn and Kinder Scout, along with an excellent perspective of the shapely peak of Shutlingsloe rising above Wildboarclough. By contrast, to the west lies the broad sweep of the Cheshire Plain and beyond to the Mersey, its waters often visible as a silver strip on the distant horizon.

Shining Tor to Buxton

Continuing southeast from the summit down the constructed path, a track is crossed that comes up from the left from the Errwood Hall ruins and continues along to the Cat and Fiddle Inn. If refreshments don't beckon, a stile gives access to a path that takes you down moorland slopes into Stake Clough, and on through woods into the upper reaches of the Goyt Valley.

Beyond the narrow valley road and the young River Goyt, the heather and bracken slopes of Goyt's Moss are ascended via Berry Clough. As height is gained, the Cat and Fiddle Inn becomes visible on the skyline behind, 'a mere speck upon the topmost height of a huge long-backed hill,' according to William Croston in 1876. The steep moorland path eventually crosses Burbage Edge to join the old Macclesfield turnpike road that leads gently back to Buxton.

INFORMATION
Start/Finish: Burbage Church, Buxton GR 043728.
Distance/Time: 21km(13miles) / 6hours.
Grading: Difficult; along good tracks, lanes and moorland paths.
Maps: OS Outdoor Leisure sheet 24 White Peak Area.
Refreshments: Cat and Fiddle Inn; various pubs and cafés in Buxton.
Public Transport: Railway station at Buxton; regular bus services from surrounding conurbations.

Crossing the ridge over Cat's Tor.

Right: *Windgather Rocks.*

63

WALK 10 Lyme Park and Sponds Hill

Rural Lyme Park in the northwest corner of the Peak District is an ideal starting point for exploring the rolling landscape west of the Goyt Valley and north of the Macclesfield to Whaley Bridge road. This green, hilly area, a mixture of moorland and pastureland, provides extensive views of western Peakland from its two highest tops of Sponds Hill and Black Hill that face each other across the valley of the Todd Brook.

The main gates of Lyme Park, just west of Disley railway station, give access to the lovely park surrounding the fine old Palladian building which was the home of the Legh family from 1346 to 1946, when it was taken over by the National Trust. In more recent times the hall has become better known for its use as 'Pemberley' in the TV production of Jane Austen's *Pride and Prejudice*. The word 'lyme' is thought to have been used to describe a part or boundary of the Royal Forest and as you approach along the drive to the car park near the big house a herd of red deer is often to be seen roaming through the parkland where once they were hunted.

Lyme Park to Sponds Hill

Our route starts at the car park and heads south along the path signposted for the Gritstone Trail leading to the foot of Knight's Low. After leaving the enclosed park a path climbs the moor to isolated and conspicuous Bowstonegate Farm where there are some of the broadest vistas in the whole of the Peak District. To the west Alderley Edge pokes out into the Cheshire Plain and, far away beyond it, are the Peckforton Hills. Greater Manchester acts as a foreground for Winter Hill in Lancashire and to the northeast, the high country of Kinder Scout and Bleaklow rise up beyond the lower Goyt and Sett Valleys.

The nearby ancient Bow Stones, a pair of pillars set in a rock base on top of Park Moor overlooking Lyme Park has been a mystery for generations of historians. They are very similar to Robin Hood's Picking Rods (or Stones) near Cown Edge, 10km/6miles to the north. Suggestions of their origins vary from where local men 'picked' their future wives from the assembled maidens, to a device for bending long bows to string them easily in this once Royal Forest. They are now thought to be shafts of late Saxon crosses placed here as boundary stones.

From the Bow Stones the walk continues along a rough track passing close to Sponds Hill's 410m/1346 feet summit where there is a viewer erected in 1975 by the Council for the Protection of Rural England to mark European Architectural Heritage Year. During the gentle descent to the narrow hill road for Pott Shrigley near Brink Farm, the familiar pointed hill of Shutlingsloe can be seen ahead. A short distance left of here the main road is crossed at Charles Head where a footpath, signposted for Kettleshulme, traverses the rough hillside down to the tree-lined Todd Brook at Reed Bridge near the charming village of Kettleshulme which, until 1937, supported one of England's few candlewick mills.

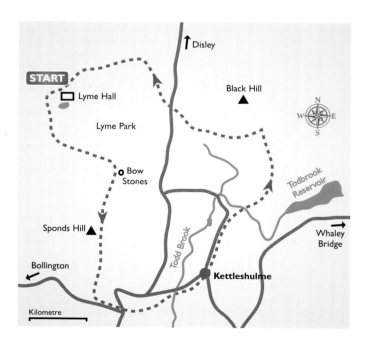

Lyme Hall.

Kettleshulme to Black Hill

From Reed Bridge the Whaley Bridge road is followed towards Kettleshulme. At the far end of the village, we fork left along Kishfield Lane that twists down into the delightful wooded valley where we cross the Todd Brook on Kishfield Bridge before climbing up the part-cobbled way to Hawkhurst Head overlooking Toddbrook Reservoir. Here, at a bend in the lane, a farm track slants up left and just after a cattle grid a path leads right up gorse banks and a pasture field before turning up left to find the old, trough-like Plague Stone.

The Plague Stone, also known as the Dipping Stone, has two sockets carved in it and is very much like the base rocks of Robin Hood's Picking Rods and the Bow Stones and until seventy-five years ago, pieces of the round shafts or uprights were still lying nearby. Clearly this was another boundary marker. At a later date the sockets are said to have been filled with vinegar where the plague-ridden folk of Disley left their money to be disinfected, just as happened in the plague village of Eyam, so others could collect it and purchase food for them.

Lyme Cage.

Looking south from Sponds Hill to Shining Tor.

66

The Todd Brook Valley.

INFORMATION
Start/Finish: Lyme Hall car park GR: 963823.
Distance/Time: 14km(9miles) / 5hours.
Grading: Easy: on mainly good tracks, foot-paths and hill roads through parkland and high moorland.
Maps: OS Outdoor Leisure sheets 1 Dark Peak Area and 24 White Peak Area.
Refreshments: Lyme Park Visitor Centre.
Public Transport: Trains and buses from Stockport and Buxton to Disley.

The Dipping Stone.

Black Hill to Lyme Park

Beyond the Stone, at a rushy hollow, you soon pick up the grassy path rising from Whaley Lane which is followed west as it contours across the southern flanks of Black Hill, before dropping through marshy ground to join the limestone track leading to the drive of nearby Moorside Hotel. The hotel drive leads to the road which is crossed to Cock-knoll Farm, beyond which fields are descended past a ruined farm to the East Lodge of Lyme Hall. From the lodge, the road can be followed back through the park to Lyme Hall with broad views over Stockport and Manchester. The conspicuous and recently-restored Lyme Cage on Cage Hill, resembling the Hunting Tower at Chatsworth, was built in 1525 and was most likely erected for the ladies of the Hall to watch the progress of the deer hunt.

THE WYE VALLEY AREA

Rising near the spa town of Buxton, the youthful River Wye rushes through Wye Dale, Chee Dale, Miller's Dale and Monsal Dale gathering dignity and charm as it meanders past the ancient walls of Haddon Hall, where it is joined by the River Lathkill, finally merging with the River Derwent at Rowsley; a relatively short journey, but a full one.

The Wye Valley is a typical limestone dale with its clear river overhung by rocky outcrops and steep woodlands rich in wildlife and flowers, while its high, open pastures are dotted with grey-stone villages. It is also a valley recovering from industrial exploitation, for its water power was harnessed to run the mills of Miller's Dale; many of its trees were thinned out to provide fuel and quarrying took its toll. In the nineteenth century, Midland Railway engineers forced a line through the heart of the valley, building a series of long tunnels and viaducts, the one at Monsal Head being the most impressive and the one which greatly upset the poet Ruskin, a great lover of the Wye Valley.

Originally built to link Buxton and Manchester with Matlock and the Midlands, the rail link survived for over a hundred years before its closure in 1968. However, feasibility studies are being undertaken by Peak Rail Ltd. to see whether the line could be re-opened for steam trains and passengers.

Despite all these sacrifices to the needs of the time, the valley has made a remarkable recovery. Grass and wild flowers creep across the ballast tracks and stations at Miller's Dale and Monsal Dale are now closed, but the old railway track is part of the Monsal Trail, stretching from Chee Dale to southeast of Bakewell.

Although the areas around the confluence of the Wye and Derwent are still strictly within the White Peak, a great boss of millstone grit rises to the southwest of Rowsley, covering the older limestone across to the River Bradford and the northern end of Gratton Dale. Here are to be found stretches of heather moorland and a number of unusual gritstone outcrops. More importantly, the moors of Stanton and Harthill to the south of Youlgreave, with their prehistoric network of trackways and ancient sites, enshrine much of the ancient history of the Peak District.

The entrance to Chee Dale.

Right: *The east end of Miller's Dale below Cressbrook seen from the Monsal Trail.*

WALK 11 Chelmorton and the Wye Valley

This walk along the most rugged sections of the Wye Valley, including some of the quiet side dales and tributaries, passes through some of the finest river scenery in the Peak District. Then, by returning across the limestone plateau to the south, via the upland villages of Taddington and Chelmorton, this circular outing gives a fascinating introduction to some quiet parts of the White Peak, including the option of a visit to the Five Wells Neolithic chambered tomb overlooking the Wye.

Wye Dale to Chee Tor

Our walk starts a little way outside Buxton at the Wye Dale car park beside the busy A6 Buxton to Bakewell road, which is also the start of the Monsal Trail. A wide riverside track, flanked by woods of ash and sycamore where in summer the air is rich with the scent of wild garlic, leads to a group of cottages on the banks of the Wye. From the narrow footbridge that crosses the river you get a spectacular view into Chee Dale with its dramatic rock architecture with huge, tree-capped limestone buttresses overhanging the narrow dale. Guarding the entrance to the dale is the massive, bulging crag of Plum Buttress.

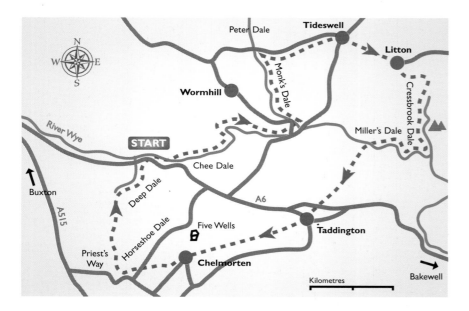

The left bank of the river is followed for much of the way and our first obstacle is where the dale narrows and the river flows between steep limestone cliffs. A series of stepping-stones which pass under a bulging rock wall is the only way through the gorge and, if the river is in spate, this section can be avoided along the disused railway track.

Stepping stones allow progress through the narrows of Chee Dale.

Eventually the river passes through another rocky gorge which is bypassed over a couple of rustic bridges, before arriving at some more stepping stones below a damp cliff. Just beyond here, by a bend in the river, you can gaze across to the imposing cliff of Chee Tor, a spectacular place that has drawn climbers, photographers and walkers for many years.

Right: *Chee Dale. The old railway track and tunnel are clearly seen.*

Beyond Chee Tor, green meadows and woodlands lead easily to the bridge at Miller's Dale where a narrow riverside road is followed towards the Angler's Rest Inn. Just before the inn, a path beside a church on the left, gives access into the Derbyshire Dales National Nature Reserve of Monk's Dale. A path meanders up through the wooded dale which in springtime bursts into a pageant of colour with its limestone-loving plants such as the Nottingham catchfly, bloody cranesbill and dog's mercury. Beyond a rocky defile the valley opens up at a narrow hill road that climbs towards Tideswell, but this is soon quitted right for a walled lane from where a path gives a pleasant stroll through walled fields into Tideswell.

Tideswell to Litton Mill

Although Tideswell is little more than a large village it boasts the magnificent fourteenth-century parish church of St John the Baptist. Known as the 'Cathedral of the Peak', the splendour of the church with its grand, Perpendicular-style pinnacled tower, is a reminder of the days when the village was of considerable importance. It was granted the right to hold a weekly market as early as the mid-thir-teenth century. Like many other White Peak villages, Tideswell con-tinues the ancient tradition of well dressings.

To the east, reached along a narrow road, is the village of Litton, meaning 'farm on the hill' with its cluster of houses, village green and the Red Lion Inn. Leaving the village by a side lane just beyond the inn, the way ahead crosses the ancient strip fields and down the dry Tansley Dale where stepping stones cross a stream into Cressbrook Dale, one of the most attractive of the Wye tributaries. Its upper section is open and contains the detached limestone outcrop of Peter's Stone, while its lower part is wooded, much of it now a National Nature Reserve above which stands the imposing buttresses of Ravensdale Crag, another favourite with rock climbers.

From the terraced row of cottages below the crag, a road climbs out of the valley and descends southwards to Cressbrook Mill, where the Wye is rejoined at the sheltered valley of Water-cum-Jolly Dale. The mill was built by Richard Arkwright and later taken over by William Newton, who employed children as labourers. Unlike those at Litton Mill further up the valley, they were said to have been well- treated. This impressive Georgian mill is now being restored and transformed into flats.

Chee Tor.

Between these two mills a concessionary path runs alongside the river, overlooked by steeply wooded slopes dotted with numerous cliffs including, Rubicon Wall, which overhangs the path, and The Cornice, a huge petrified wave of limestone suspended above the river on the opposite bank. In summer, a profusion of wild flowers and the gentle murmuring waters welcome you, but after periods of heavy rain the valley is prone to flooding and may be impassable. Then the Monsal Trail traversing the far side of the dale can be used.

The riverside path ends suddenly at Litton Mill, which began life as a cotton mill in the late-eighteenth century and was made infamous by the owner, Ellis Needham, and his harsh exploitation of child labourers, many of whom died and were buried at Tideswell. The mill has been derelict for some years and is now being converted into holiday cottages.

Litton Mill to Chelmorton

From Litton Mill cottages, a footbridge crosses the Wye to a steep track leading up past the Monsal Trail, then through scrubby pastures and fields, eventually crossing High Dale and the A6 road to reach the ancient, linear village of Taddington. Taddington looks north across Miller's Dale towards the heights of Kinder Scout, while to the west are the walled pastures of Taddington Moor which our route crosses for Chelmorton along a series of footpaths and tracks.

Between the two villages, just north of Fivewells Farm and approached by a detour along a concessionary path, is the Five Wells chambered cairn monument. This Neolithic tomb, built between 4500 and 2000 BC, has extensive views over the Wye valley to the north and standing at over 430m/1200ft, is thought to be one of the highest chambered tombs in England. The grass-covered cairn of limestone rubble, raised over two stone burial chambers, has revealed much information about the Neolithic period in the White Peak.

Rubicon Wall, Water-cum-Jolly.

Chelmorton, which is little more than a single street of grey farm buildings and cottages, and standing at 365m/1200ft above sea level, is the highest village in Derbyshire. As with Taddington, the landscape around Chelmorton is of historic importance in that the parallel, stone-walled fields which spread back either side of the village, preserve the outline of strip fields of medieval times.

Chelmorton Low, its summit crowned by a pair of Bronze Age tumuli, overlooks the village, and from its slopes a stream flows down through the village and bears the quaint name of Illy Willy Water. From the middle of the village, beyond the splendid thirteenth-century church, a path leads westwards through walled fields to join a road. Just along the road to the west, beyond Farditch Farm, Horseshoe Dale is entered on the right. The path soon becomes Priest's Way, an ancient track linking the monastic granges of Brierlow Bar and King Sterndale. Horseshoe Dale merges into wild and rugged Deep Dale where Black Dale comes in from the left. Deep Dale is rich in wild flowers especially around Thurst House Cave, beyond which the narrow dale leads down past the spoil heaps and slurry ponds of Topley Pike Quarry to the A6 road opposite Wye Dale car park.

INFORMATION
Start/Finish: Wye Dale car park GR 104725.
Distance/Time: 25km(16miles) / 8hours.
Grading: Difficult; mainly along good paths and tracks through sheltered dales and breezy uplands.
Maps: OS Outdoor Leisure sheet 24 White Peak Area.
Refreshments: The Angler's Rest, Miller's Dale; pubs and cafés in Tideswell; the Red Lion, Litton; the Queen's Arms, Taddington; the Church Inn, Chelmorton.
Public Transport: Regular bus service between Buxton and Bakewell.

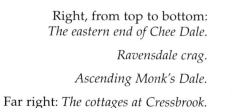

Right, from top to bottom:
The eastern end of Chee Dale.

Ravensdale crag.

Ascending Monk's Dale.

Far right: *The cottages at Cressbrook.*

WALK 12 Monsal Dale and Magpie Mine

Monsal Dale, with its famous railway viaduct spanning the valley, is best seen from the scenic viewpoint at Monsal Head, which stands high above an expansive loop in the Wye Valley. The silver thread of the river weaves its way towards Ashford-in-the-Water, gliding between Fin Cop and Putwell Hill beside meadows enriched with wild flowers, willow, hawthorn and mountain ash.

The narrow road which links Monsal Head with Ashford has existed for centuries and was part of the Saxon ridgeway known as the Portway, one of the most ancient highways in Derbyshire. The Portway joined the River Wye at Ashford's seventeenth-century Sheepwash Bridge. Originally a packhorse bridge it replaced the ford of the Portway and as its name implies, is the oldest and most picturesque bridge across the Wye, with a pen next to it where sheep were washed prior to shearing.

It is here at Sheepwash Bridge where this varied circular walk starts, visiting the former lead mining village of Sheldon. The route then passes through Deep Dale and Monsal Dale, finally returning across the lime-stone plateau to the village of Ashford. It passes through a placid landscape which belies its rich historical and industrial heritage.

Ashford to Sheldon

Ashford-in-the-Water is a sleepy little village, known for its well-dressings held early in June. Just along the A6 from Sheepwash Bridge, a minor road leads left up to Sheldon through Kirk Dale and is left at a bend in the road past an old quarry where Ashford Black Marble was mined in the eighteenth and nineteenth centuries. Not a true marble, this polished dark grey limestone was very popular for ornamental and inlay work, and used in both Hardwick Hall and Chatsworth. The square-towered Norman church of Holy Trinity in Ashford has interesting examples of black marble inside.

A riverside-track beside the Wye can be followed towards the partly-restored bobbin mills beneath Great Shacklow Wood, and are well worth a visit. Here, bobbins were made for the local cotton mills such as Cressbrook. Our route leaves the pastures before reaching the mills and ascends a path through Little Shacklow Wood to enter the charming, single-street farming village of Sheldon.

Sheldon is a typical limestone village, once a mining settlement where the work of extracting lead ore from nearby mines and rakes coexisted with farming. There are few important relics from those days but just south of the village, approached by field paths, is Magpie Mine that started extracting lead as early as the seventeenth century and continued working into the 1950s. Its preserved remains, now a field study centre run by the Peak District Mines Historical Society, are one of the best examples of old lead mine workings in the area and make an interesting diversion. The Cornish engine house, with its distinctive round Cornish chimney, looks impressive silhouetted against a setting sun. In early summer you find lovely displays of lead-tolerant plants such as the white-flowered spring sandwort, known locally as leadwort, and clumps of mountain pansies on the lead spoil heaps.

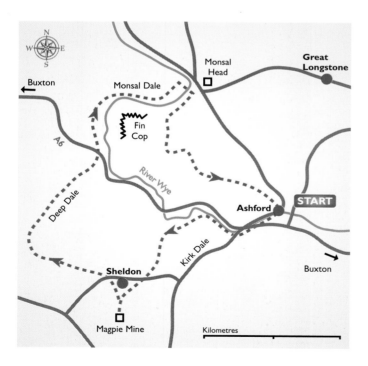

The seventeenth-century Sheepwash Bridge, Ashford-in-the-Water.

Sheldon to Monsal Head

Returning in the steps of the 't'owd Man' – as lead miners are called – across fields to the western end of Sheldon, a footpath leads west through a series of walled pastures into the head of Deep Dale which is descended. This dry valley, with wooded slopes on its northern flanks and open scrubland on the opposite side, was worked for lead and the series of hollows in the upper reaches denote old mine shafts. In springtime the lower slopes of the dale are carpeted with early purple orchids and cowslips. After dropping down through a rocky defile known as Demon's Dell, you pass through the White Lodge car park and cross the busy A6 road to enter beautiful, wooded Monsal Dale.

A great promontory commands the eastern entrance to the valley forcing the Wye to follow a huge curve around its lower flanks. Known as Fin Cop, this steep-sided hill is crowned by an Iron Age Hill Fort. Although the right of way path is away from the river, most walkers amble along the grassy riverbank to a weir, just beyond which the impressive 25m (80ft) high railway viaduct with its five stone arches spanning the gorge, fills the skyline. Erected in 1867 to carry the Midland Railway line to Buxton, the viaduct is a fine memorial to the engineers who designed and built it.

Not everybody loved the railway and viaduct, though, and it incurred the wrath of the poet Ruskin, a great admirer of the Wye Valley. He wrote: 'The valley is gone and now every fool in Buxton can be in Bakewell in half an hour and every fool in Bakewell at Buxton; which you think a lucrative process of exchange – you Fools everywhere'. Ironically the Monsal Dale viaduct is now a listed and protected structure and a valued part of our industrial heritage.

A path climbs left through scrubland up to a gate giving access to the Monsal Trail which passes airily over the viaduct, at the end of which a woodland path traverses the hillside up to Monsal Head. William Adam, writing in his mid-nineteenth century guidebook, 'Gem of the Peak', describes how he visited this point with a friend who was astonished and asked, 'What is this place? Surely this is second paradise!' It might not be that quite today, but it is still one of the most popular beauty spots in Derbyshire.

The Wye flows over weirs below Great Shacklow Wood.

The old railway viaduct at Monsal Head.

Right: *Magpie Mine.*

Below right: *White flowered sandwort, known locally as leadwort, found on the old lead spoil heaps of Magpie Mine.*

Monsal Head to Ashford

From this high vantage point you get a marvellous view westwards over the famous viaduct to the bold escarpment of Fin Cop and north along the picturesque, upper dale towards Cressbrook. It is along these gentle pastures that the River Wye calms down after its dash through the limestone gorges of Chee Dale and Miller's Dale to the north, before continuing sedately under the viaduct, through Monsal Dale and on to Bakewell. On summer days, the picnic tables outside the Monsal Head Inn provide a welcome break in the walk to sit and admire this fine White Peak landscape.

To get back to Ashford, we traverse the top edge of the wooded flanks of Monsal Dale towards Fin Cop along a path overlooking the craggy landslip known as Hob's House. The walk soon swings south through walled fields via tracks and lanes leading down into the village.

WALK 13   Lathkill Dale

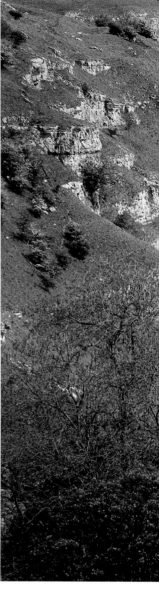

Lathkill Dale, stretching for about 10km/6miles from Monyash to Alport, is arguably one of the most beautiful limestone valleys in the Peak District. The dale contains wooded hillsides rich in a diversity of plant life, weirs, sparkling waters, limestone cliffs and old mine workings, relics from a bygone age when the dale was a hive of industrial activity although today the remains are softened by Nature.

Starting from the plateau village of Monyash, this circular walk follows Lathkill Dale to the confluence of the Lathkill with the Alport, from where our return journey starts along the wooded Bradford Dale, then traverses the broad, limestone tableland to finish back at Monyash.

Monyash, just east of the main Buxton to Ashbourne road, is a typical limestone village of stone-built cottages and farms, clustered around the church and village green. Although the village is now involved with tourism and farming, it was once an important mining centre with its own Barmote Court, which controlled the local lead mining industry. The village was granted its market charter in 1340 and the old market cross still stands at the centre of the village green near the Bull's Head. In the fourteenth and fifteenth centuries, an ancient right of way from Derby to Manchester linked the surrounding villages and later still, packhorses carried salt from Cheshire to Bakewell and Chesterfield along a trail just south of the village.

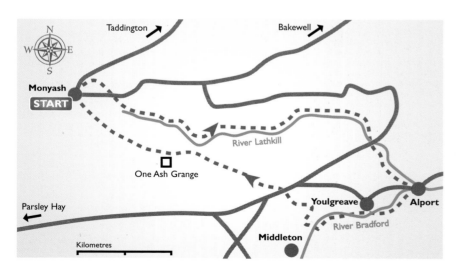

Apart from the obvious attractions of the limestone dales scenery passed during the walk, it is the remarkable clarity of the waters of the River Lathkill on its short but fascinating journey to Alport that remains in the memory. The seventeenth-century fishing guru, Charles Cotton, described the river as, '… the purest, the most transparent stream that I ever yet saw…'.

Monyash to Alport

Heading north out of the village and bearing right at a junction, the path leads right down the shallow dry valley of Bagshaw Dale. This is quite a short dale and once the B5055 Bakewell Road has been crossed, you enter Lathkill Dale proper. Initially the dale is shallow and grassy, but soon becomes narrow, tree-lined and rocky at the site of the former Ricklow Quarry, where the path hugs the right hand slopes of the gorge to negotiate a boulder field. The quarry yielded grey limestone rich in sea lily fossils (or crinoids), which was polished to produce 'figured marble' popular in Victorian times.

Up to now the dale has been dry and usually remains so until Lathkill Head Cave is reached on the right. From this resurgence cave, the clear waters of the Lathkill emerge in wet weather, lending life and interest to the surroundings. The water flows over a carpet of vegetation that hints at the river's unusual habit during prolonged periods of dry weather of disappearing underground to continue on its eastward course, resurfacing further downstream beyond Lathkill Lodge.

Beyond the entrance to the Derbyshire Dales National Nature Reserve the now treeless, steep-sided dale opens up and is joined on the left by another dry dale overlooked by the impressive limestone crag of Parson's Tor. The path hugs the left bank of the slow-moving river as it

Ahead the dale closes in again as the path passes through Palmerston Woods, the tree-cloaked hillsides emphasising the narrowness of the dale. The trees manage to mask the scars of the industrial relics left behind from lead mining. The remains of the Mandale Mine, one of the oldest mines in the Peak District, is soon passed on the left. On a peaceful autumn day here it is difficult to imagine this enchanting area echoing to the sound of mine working.

The river now takes on a gentler character as it flows serenely past Lathkill Lodge, over a series of weirs and under the medieval, narrow Conksbury Bridge, an old packhorse crossing on the Bakewell to Youlgreave road. A short distance up the narrow road to the right the path, now on the southern side of the river, is rejoined, crossing fields as it runs parallel to the River Lathkill, and soon leads into the hamlet of Alport. Situated at the junction of the Bradford and Lathkill rivers, Alport has some lovely seventeenth- and eighteenth-century cottages.

Alport to Monyash

Along the road just west of Alport, a footbridge over the River Bradford leads down to the left to join a riverside path passing below the limestone cliffs of Rheinstor, beyond which the houses of Youlgreave come into view, ranged up the northern slopes above the river. The village makes a pleasant detour for refreshments.

follows the huge bends in the valley, passing a footbridge on the right that provides access to the wooded confines of Cales Dale.

Lathkill Dale is beautiful in all seasons but particularly in spring when the craggy slopes are a profusion of cowslips and the natural ash woods, are rich with bluebells, red campion and many other species; while dippers are often to be seen in the river.

The walk continues along the riverside footpath through Bradford Dale, changing banks several times over bridges. The dale provides pleasant walking through a sheltered landscape of wooded slopes overlooking a series of weirs and ponds. This dale was described in 1905 by J.B. Frith as containing, '… still pools even more crystal clear than those of Lathkill.'

After crossing a stone bridge a steep track zigzags up through woodland to the Middleton-Youlgreave road which is followed right past Lomberdale Hall. A path at the next bend leads up across another minor road, from where walled pastures take you up to Moor Lane car park and picnic site. Ahead is the broad limestone plateau at the heart of the White Peak.

The return journey to Monyash follows part of the Limestone Way; an excellent 42km/26miles walk linking Matlock and Castleton. Walled pastureland is crossed on a good footpath skirting Calling Low Farm on the right through several small wooded enclosures. Continuing across the high pastures on a good footpath you soon descend the stepped path into the rocky ravine of Cales Dale, a side valley rising up from the depths of Lathkill Dale.

After crossing the dale a steep path climbs up through the wood eventually arriving at a Dutch barn on the edge of One Ash Grange, founded in medieval times and one of the oldest farms in the area. Originally a penitentiary farmstead for monks, One Ash Grange was owned by Roche Abbey in South Yorkshire and provided the abbey with wool from the sheep that occupied the large pastures around the grange. The buildings still exude great antiquity, especially the ancient pig stys you pass behind the farm.

Beyond the grange, a farm track leads west towards Fern Dale, a side valley off Lathkill Dale. The dry dale is crossed through walled fields to join another farm lane leading to Monyash, its church steeple an obvious landmark in the open landscape.

The upper section of Lathkill Dale.

INFORMATION
Start/Finish: Monyash car park GR: 150667.
Distance/Time: 19km(12miles) / 5hours.
Grading: Moderate; through limestone dales and across pastureland.
Maps: OS Outdoor Leisure sheet 24 White Peak Area.
Refreshments: Various cafés and pubs in Youlgreave; the Bull's Head and café in Monyash.
Public Transport: Buses from Buxton and Bakewell.

The River Lathkill flows through the picturesque hamlet of Alport.

Left: *Waterfall in upper Lathkill Dale.*

Right: *The narrow, twisting section of Lathkill Dale upstream from Conksbury.*

WALK 14 Harthill and Stanton Moors

The charming village of Youlgreave is an ideal base for exploring some of the most fascinating archaeological features of the White Peak. Youlgreave sits on a shelf of land overlooking the River Bradford and is surrounded by pastures criss-crossed by limestone walls. It is also a landscape cut by deep river valleys like Lathkill and Bradford Dales.

These limestone uplands were some of the first places in the area to be settled and today are a fascinating source of prehistoric remains. One of the most important of these is the Neolithic stone circle of Arbor Low on Middleton Moor, between the valleys of the Bradford and Lathkill. Similarly the rolling landscape south of Youlgreave, which is a contrasting mixture of limestone and gritstone pastures, also shows much evidence of past civilisations including barrows, stone circles, earthworks, lead mines and ancient byways, including the Portway, a prehistoric trackway.

Youlgreave to Cratcliffe Tor

Youlgreave, one of the largest villages in this part of the White Peak, is a fascinating place with some impressive seventeenth-century buildings and one of the most delightful churches in the area. The parish church of All Saints has a fine Perpendicular tower and wide Norman nave.

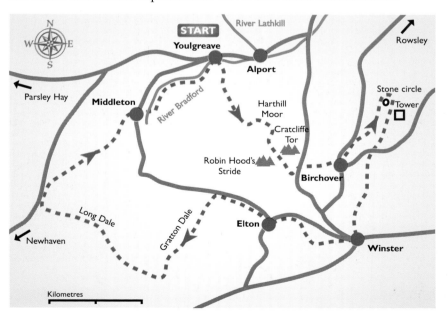

Starting beside the great west tower of Youlgreave church, the way heads steeply down to the edge of the village, then across the River Bradford, to follow the Limestone Way through pastures climbing up to Round Wood. The wall-capped hill-top ahead is the prehistoric earthwork of Castle Ring, a small Iron Age hill-fort. Harthill Moor Farm is bypassed to the north along a track curving through a conifer plantation, to reach the narrow hill road linking Alport and Elton. This is the line of the Portway that passes close to the burial mounds on nearby Stanton Moor and the stone circle on Harthill Moor, our next objective.

Beyond the lane, fields are crossed to the prominent collection of eroded gritstone pinnacles of Robin Hood's Stride, a delightful spot surrounded by trees and so named because the legendary figure of Robin is supposed to have stepped across the gap between them. When silhouetted at dusk it is easy to see why these rocks long ago earned the title of Mock Beggar's Hall. From here you get excellent views northwards to the wooded hills above Haddon Hall and Chatsworth. Just across pastureland to the north are the four remaining standing stones from the original Nine Stones Circle – one of the best prehistoric monuments in this part of the Peak District and second only to Arbor Low.

Opposite Robin Hood's Stride, the gritstone rocks of Cratcliffe Tor rise above bracken and wooded slopes and are easily reached along a footpath. Hidden at the foot of the rocks, behind some ancient yews, is the Hermit's Cave with its carved seat, crucifix and lamp niche. Various hermits, who were respected holy men, are thought to have occupied this simple rock shelter during the Middle Ages. It was certainly occupied in 1549 when written evidence describes how a hermit had supplied five rabbits to Haddon Hall. From the top of the rocks you can gaze eastwards over Birchover to Stanton Moor.

From Robin Hood's Stride, the Portway, now a track with bedrock and rough paving stones, leads down to the B5056 road which is followed north for a short distance to where a footpath climbs across fields with fine views back across to Cratcliffe Tor. You eventually arrive at the conspicuous conical hillock of Rowter Rocks with its tiny Jesus Chapel, on the edge of Birchover village. These fascinating rocks, shaded by old trees, have rooms, stairs, alcoves and chairs which were carved out by the local vicar, the Rev. Thomas Eyre in the early-eighteenth century, and are a delight to explore.

The rocks of Cratcliffe Tor dominate the skyline of Harthill Moor.

Birchover to Winster

Some of the fine seventeenth- and eighteenth-century cottages that line the main road though Birchover are made from finely grained gritstone quarried at the edge of Stanton Moor. From the Druid's Inn, adjacent to Rowter Rocks, a path climbs northeast, crosses the Stanton–Birchover road, and passes to the left of the still active gritstone quarry to arrive at Stanton Moor. At the top, near the triangulation point, stands the huge curious boulder of the Cork Stone. This natural rock has carved footholds and hand rings to assist its ascent.

Though Stanton Moor is of modest area it is remarkable for its density of ancient relics and contains one of the finest collections of Late Neolithic and Early Bronze Age remains in Britain. Here are to be found numerous cairns and barrows scattered over the heather moor, alongside stone circles and standing stones. The father and son team of J.C. and J.P. Heathcote excavated many of the sites and established a private museum in Birchover. Since its closure, many of the relics they found are now in Weston Park Museum in Sheffield.

By continuing across the moor on a broad track you arrive at the ring of low stones of the Nine Ladies Stone Circle. Set in a clearing among birch trees, this ring of low stones, with the King Stone lying just to the west, dates from the Bronze Age and is still a popular venue for New Age visitors.

Returning along the eastern brink of the moor, we pass The Stand, a prominent stone tower erected as a tribute to Earl Charles Grey, the prime minister who introduced the Parliamentary Reform Bill in 1832. From here there is an expansive view of the Derwent Valley, before you head south, crossing the lane linking Stanton Lees with Birchover, to follow a path across pastureland to eventually enter the village of Winster.

Top right: *Nine Ladies Stone Circle, Stanton Moor.*

Right: *Remaining standing stones from the original Nine Stones Circle, Harthill Moor.*

Winster to Youlgreave

Winster is one of the oldest and most picturesque villages in the Peak District and was once the centre of the local lead mining industry. West of the village a path leads through woodland and fields to join the line of the Portway and the newer Limestone Way, which can be followed towards the village of Elton with its seventeenth- and eighteenth-century houses. A settlement appears to have existed here since early Saxon times, but from Roman times, lead has been extracted in the vicinity. The village also sits on a geological boundary between gritstone and limestone, which explains why the two different building materials have been used along the main street.

The village is surrounded by uplands through which our walk passes northwest to Dale End and the entrance to Gratton Dale. This little-known, dry limestone valley, a sanctuary for wildlife, has an enclosed atmosphere, its scrubby slopes precluding any views of the countryside beyond. In the winter months after prolonged rain the lower half of Gratton Dale can be very wet and muddy. At the end of the dale, past some boulders and elder scrub, the path turns right into grassy Long Dale which makes easy walking.

On reaching the busy Newhaven-Youlgreave road the way is northwards for a few hundred metres to where a footpath strikes right across fields to join the narrow Whitfield Lane leading to Middleton-by-

Youlgreave. The lane provides a grand prospect across Calton Pastures, the Eastern Edges and Stanton Moor. Middleton-by-Youlgreave with its stone farms and cottages is a quiet, leafy place standing back from a junction of lanes, with Middleton Hall hidden behind tall trees.

From the centre of the village a track descends through a tree-cloaked limestone gorge into the narrow wooded confines of Bradford Dale. High above the western flanks at this end of the dale stands Lomberdale Hall, the former home of Thomas Bateman the archaeologist who excavated numerous Peak District barrows in the 1840s and 1850s.

As you walk back to Youlgreave through this sheltered landscape of wooded slopes overlooking a series of weirs and ponds, you can easily agree with the claim made at the beginning of the twentieth century that, 'for peaceful loveliness and sheer prettiness, nothing in Derbyshire excels this little limestone gorge'.

Silver birch wood on Stanton Moor.

INFORMATION
Start/Finish: Youlgreave GR: 211644.
Distance/Time: 23km(15miles) / 7hours.
Grading: Difficult; an undulating walk on mainly good footpaths and tracks through limestone dales and across heather moorland and limestone pastures.
Maps: OS Outdoor Leisure sheet 24 White Peak Area.
Refreshments: Plenty of pubs and cafés in Youlgreave including the George Hotel and the Farmyard; the Druids Inn at Birchover; Miner's Standard at Winster.
Public Transport: Buses from Bakewell, Chesterfield, Matlock and Buxton.

The eastern end of Long Dale.

The River Bradford near Youlgreave.

Below left: *The roughly-paved Portway climbing up to Robin Hood's Stride.*

Below: *Cork Stone, Stanton Moor.*

WALK 15 Over Calton Pastures to Chatsworth

Between Bakewell and Chatsworth is an area of gentle hills and valleys, magnificently wooded and still showing the results of enlightened management by wealthy nobility through many centuries. No British stately homes stand in finer countryside than Chatsworth and Haddon Hall, both of which are seen along this pleasant walk that crosses the high, wood-flanked ridge to the east of Bakewell. A good day out at any time of year.

The small but busy town of Bakewell, situated on the River Wye, has one of the oldest markets in the area dating from 1254 and markets are still held here every Monday. There is a thriving livestock market in a modern Agricultural Business Centre across the Wye. Evidence of Bakewell's ancient origins are found in the collection of Saxon carved stones and two impressive crosses at the hillside parish church of All Saints. The Peak District National Park also has its headquarters in Bakewell.

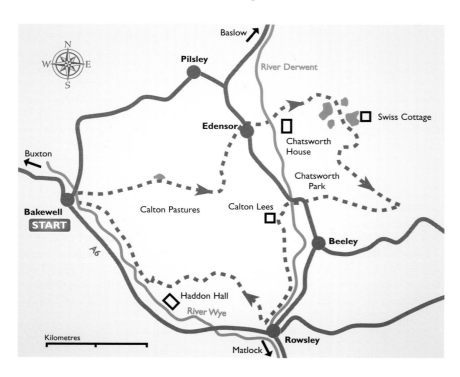

Bakewell to Chatsworth

Starting from Bakewell's ancient fourteenth-century bridge over the River Wye, the route turns right into Coombs Road and then left opposite the entrance to the showground up a track. After crossing the bridge over the former Midland Railway – now the Monsal Trail – you ascend diagonally right across the golf course into Manners Wood, which in springtime is carpeted in bluebells. Just before entering the trees, a fine prospect back over Bakewell opens up. After climbing the steep path through the wood the great prairie expanse of Calton Pastures at 274m/900feet above sea level is reached, the highest part of the route.

Passing a pond the walk advances towards the Derwent Valley – in summer this broad, sweeping section of pasture has the feel of downland, especially so if you hear the bleating of the Chatsworth flocks. Aiming for Russian Cottage, a compliment to the 6th Duke of Devonshire's friendship with the Tsar of Russia, the way soon turns left into New Piece Wood by a Dutch barn and comes into the open sward of Chatsworth Park.

Today's park was created largely in the eighteenth century by the 4th Duke under the direction of that fine landscape gardener, Capability Brown, and the public road (B6012) now seen below was made about 1770. The enlightened Dukes of Devonshire have allowed people to wander in the park for many, many years and the signboard here shows the area of public access. Descending to Edensor (pronounced Ensor) village, its tall church spire an easy marker, you may be lucky and see herds of fallow or red deer, certainly you'll be unlucky if pheasants aren't roaming on the grass.

Top right: *Pond on Calton Pastures.*

Right: *Calton Pastures.*

Edensor to Calton Lees

Edensor, Chatsworth's remarkable estate village where no two houses have the same design, was removed here between 1838 and 1842 from a site nearer the great house. Passing through the village, we come over the ridge to see suddenly ahead the 'Palace of the Peak'. The present magnificent mansion was rebuilt during the period 1678–1707 over the original mid-sixteenth century home of Bess of Hardwick and her husband William Cavendish. Many people have stayed here but the most famous was probably the imprisoned Mary, Queen of Scots.

Across the bridge over the Derwent the way goes northeast up the slopes to a point where the concessionary footpath from Baslow comes southeast, then up through steep woods to pass near the Hunting Tower; a look-out for Bess of Hardwick. The northern tip of the Emperor Lake is skirted on the way to Swiss Lake with its fanciful cottage on the far shore, and so along the track through plantations and rhododendrons, crossing Park Farm drive to pass out of the walled section onto the moor edge. Ahead lies Beeley Hilltop with its large, early-seventeenth-century farmhouse and broad views to the man-made landscape across the Derwent Valley, which we visited earlier in the day.

Heading diagonally down the moorside, a walled track is joined leading westwards to Beeley Hilltop. The walk now continues down the lane, past Beeley Lodge, to the road crossing over the Derwent and so to the Chatsworth Garden Centre with its café, and the stone hamlet of Calton Lees, an outlying estate settlement. Just beyond the last farm a good, signposted field path for Rowsley goes southwards through level grassland below Lindop Wood. Across the river to the east stands the squat tower of St Anne's church at Beeley, backed by the skyline of the Eastern Moors.

Rowsley to Bakewell

Rowsley's cottages and farms are finally reached after passing through an arch under the defunct Midland Railway. High above the village to the north sits Rowsley Moor Wood which can be easily approached up the steepening lane from where the lower Wye Valley is readily seen, with just a suggestion of the broad limestone heights of the White Peak beyond.

The way ahead was the original road between Bakewell and Rowsley and is followed as it meanders through undulating wooded countryside from where you can pause to admire the pastoral scene towards Bakewell, before continuing down to Bowling Green Farm with its unusual house. The Haddon tunnel of the Midland Railway just beyond is crossed at its northern portal. The tunnel was a prerequisite of the Duke of Rutland's permission for the railway company to bring the main line up the valley so close to Haddon Hall and here, from the tunnel-top, we get the only reasonable view of Haddon Hall, the most complete, untouched medieval castle-cum-manor house in England.

Haddon Hall.

After descending the surfaced road, a bridleway then a footpath lead pleasantly through riverside meadows on the eastern banks of the Wye, back to Bakewell and the end of the walk.

Bowling Green Farm

Bowling Green Farm is a little known architectural gem high above Haddon Hall overlooking the lowermost Wye Valley. Built just before the Rutlands abandoned their great house at the beginning of the eighteenth century, it was maintained later in the century by the family for the 'pleasure of the gentlemen of Bakewell and the neighbourhood' – most of them being Rutland tenants. The bowling green itself is surrounded by a beautifully proportioned stone wall shaded by yew trees. The southwestern side has a broad, stone staircase and iron gates opening onto the green. Opposite, on the far side, is the large, stone pavilion which is now a most unusual Derbyshire farmhouse. In 1816 Ebenezer Rhodes, the travel writer, described the place as 'totally neglected' but today's walker passing beside the high wall will see a well-preserved house and level lawn, with the old avenue of trees leading steeply down towards the back of Haddon Hall.

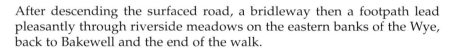

INFORMATION
Start/Finish: Bakewell.
Distance/Time: 21km(13miles) / 7hours.
Grading: Moderate; along footpaths, tracks and roads through woodlands and open parkland.
Maps: OS Outdoor Leisure sheet 24 White Peak Area.
Refreshments: Bakewell; Chatsworth Carriage Restaurant (when Chatsworth House is open); Chatsworth Garden Centre, Calton Lees; Caudwell's Mill, Rowsley.
Public Transport: Buses from Buxton, Sheffield, Chesterfield and Derby to Bakewell.

Chatsworth – the Palace of the Peak.

DERWENT VALLEY AND THE EASTERN EDGES

The great, gritstone backbone that runs southwards from the Langsett Moors near Penistone to the vicinity of Matlock and Crich, acts as a boundary rampart between the gentler coal measure country and the bulk of rugged Peakland proper. Known as the Eastern Moors, this vast area contains impressive craggy escarpments like those at Stanage and Curbar which face west, catching the evening sunshine. From their rough, gritstone buttresses steep slopes, strewn with boulder fields and occasional tree cover, lead down to the Derwent Valley and village communities such as Baslow and Curbar. To the east, broad plains of bleak heather and moor grass tilt gently to the hidden, wooded corners of Sheffield's Mayfield Valley and to the Cordwell, Linacre and the Amber Valleys.

Sections of these wide dip slopes are used for water gathering in numerous reservoirs, while the rocks themselves have been a playground for generations of climbers. Along the highest ground prehistoric people sited burial mounds and stone circles, as on Big Moor and Eyam Moor, including the important Bronze Age sites at Swine Sty and Barbrook. The Medieval trackways which cross the moor are still marked by stone guide posts.

These moorlands offer feelings of great space akin to those generated on Kinder Scout and Bleaklow. The green lowlands seem a long way off in the east and the birch-dotted marshes of Leash Fen, for instance, often have the countenance of some distant Savanna-scape.

The Upper Derwent: The Drowned Valley

Rising on the Bleaklow plateau, the River Derwent flows through the Upper Derwent Valley, an ideal place for a series of reservoirs. Authorisation for this massive civil engineering project came from the Derwent Valley Water Act of 1899 and the first two dams of Howden and Derwent were completed by 1916. A railway was built to carry stone from quarries at Grindleford and a village, known as 'Tin Town' was built near Birchinlee to house the hundreds of navvies who worked on the project. Ladybower, the third of the reservoirs, took 10 years to construct, and was finally opened by King George VI in 1945. The reservoirs supply drinking water to Derby, Nottingham, Leicester and Sheffield by means of underground pipes.

Beneath the waters of Ladybower went the ancient farming communities of the twin villages of Ashopton and Derwent, the villagers being rehoused at Yorkshire Bridge near Bamford. Prior to the flooding Derwent Hall was a youth hostel and the packhorse bridge which used to stand near its gates was dismantled and rebuilt at Slippery Stones at the head of Howden Reservoir. In addition to the halls and houses went a church, Methodist chapel, the Ashopton Inn and 10 farms. During periods of severe drought, the foundations of Derwent village are still revealed. The dams are memorials to these lost villages and manage to create a pleasing landscape, quite unique in the Peak District. The National Park visitor centre at Fairholmes has a display giving the history of the development of the valley.

Although the hillsides overlooking the reservoirs are cloaked in conifer plantations, the Forestry Commission is planning to clear some of these and reinstate native woodlands. Over the next fifty years, most of the conifers on the western side of Derwent Reservoir will be carefully removed and replaced by native trees such as upland oak and birch which will encourage a greater diversity of plants and bird life.

In 1943 the valley echoed to the noise of Lancaster bombers of 617 Squadron who used Derwent Reservoir to practice the skills needed to drop Barnes Wallis's famous 'bouncing bombs' prior to the May attack on the Ruhr Valley dams. Flypasts and reunions of 617 Squadron take place regularly at the Derwent Dam.

Grindleford and the Hope Valley from Froggatt Edge.

WALK 16   Big Moor and its Eastern Edges

Included as part of a circular walk around Big Moor, the gritstone escarpments of Froggatt, Curbar, Baslow, Birchen and Gardom's lying on the eastern rim of the Derwent Valley, give one of the finest edge walks in the Peak District. This area is also rich in prehistoric sites, some of which will be seen during the walk. The popular car park at Curbar Edge, the prominent 'nick' in the skyline above the village of Calver, makes a good starting point for this delightful moorland walk. Here, where the ancient packhorse route between Chesterfield and the Derwent Valley crosses the crest of the gritstone edge, are fine views up and down Derbyshire's major valley and across to the limestone gorge of Middleton Dale.

The high point of Big Moor.

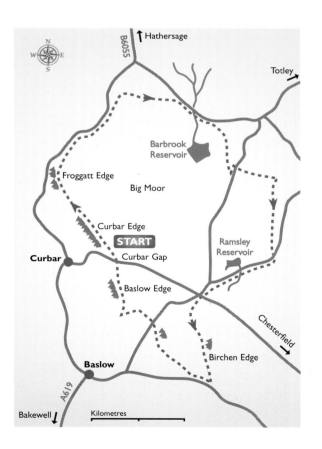

Curbar Gap to Big Moor

From the car park a gate gives access onto the moorland path along the top of Curbar Edge which offers great views, especially southwards across Baslow Edge to the wooded Chatsworth Estate. The track soon dips to a depression, from where a slight detour can be made along a path descending left below the steep rocks of Froggatt Edge, one of the Peak's most popular climbing edges. Here is to be found the detached block-shaped Froggatt Pinnacle up which goes the classic climb of Valkyrie, first ascended by Joe Brown and Wilf White in 1948.

The main edge path continues along the crest of Froggatt Edge with excellent valley views, while to the right the moorland of Stoke Flat lies beneath White Edge. If time permits seek out the small Bronze Age stone circle just off to the right where the edge and track curves north.

A broad sandy track eventually runs into silver birch woodland to join the B6054 road that leads right past the Grouse Inn. Beyond the inn a moorland path heads right, ascending towards the silhouette of White Edge Lodge, a former game-keeper's house on the Duke of Rutland's estate. Near this lonely dwelling our way is eastwards, across White Edge Moor, mounting near the skyline by way of Lady's Cross – a weathered medieval marker stone at this northern corner of Big Moor. Soon the infant Bar Brook is crossed to gain the road, midway between Owler Bar and Fox House Inn. Across Totley Moss to the north can be seen the top of the air ventilator for Totley Tunnel, the second longest in the country, on the railway line between Sheffield and Manchester.

Big Moor and White Edge overlook Curbar Edge.

Across Big Moor

Most of Big Moor, and its neighbour Ramsley Moor to the east, are part of the National Park Authority's Eastern Moors Estate and rights of way now exist across them. A concessionary path runs eastwards from near Bar Brook Bridge and keeps close beside the B6054 road to link up with the path striking southwards near Bucka Hill. Bar Brook Reservoir lies well down to the right as we follow the pleasant green lane dotted with sentinel hawthorns. The whole area around Barbrook is littered with cairns and ancient stones, including one of the best-preserved embanked stone circles in the Peak District. This circle of 12 stones on a shelf of raised ground is very similar to the Nine Ladies on Stanton Moor.

After crossing the tarmac drive and skirting rushy ground the green lane is picked up again that leads to the Sheffield – Baslow road at Car Top, from where the straight Car Lane, just across the road to the left, is followed. Ahead lies the broad sweep of the beautiful Vale of Barlow, its tilting fields divided by hedges and little woods. The walk now turns southwards to mount steadily along the fringe of wooded Ramsley Moor. The steep scarp slope to the left is Hewetts Bank, the last bastion of younger coal measures which extend east for many miles to form the Yorkshire and Derbyshire coalfields.

Reaching Fox Lane at its junction with Far Lane, at the conspicuous Shillito Plantation, the walk passes little Ramsley Reservoir before descending to join the Sheffield – Baslow road, where, from the nearby crossroads, a path crosses the moor to the popular climber's crag of Birchen Edge. Crowning the edge is the column of the Nelson Monument and the three 'battleship' tors commemorating fighting ships of the time. In fact the names of many of the rock climbs here have a nautical theme.

Top right: *Climbers reaching the summit of Froggatt Pinnacle after an ascent of the classic rock climb, Valkyrie.*

Right: *Froggatt Pinnacle. Note the millstone.*

Birchen Edge to Curbar Gap

Heading southwards below the slabby buttresses, a worn track descends to the Robin Hood Inn on the Chesterfield – Baslow road. Just down from the inn, a path heads right climbing bracken-covered slopes up to the southern end of Gardom's Edge, whose rough, gritstone buttresses overlook ancient oak and silver birch woodland. Nearby is a recently excavated Neolithic site with its extensive enclosure.

The path now contours the high side of a field before dropping down through woods to reach the A621 road near Cupola Cottage. Beyond the busy highway a footpath crosses the tumbling Bar Brook and up steeply through woodland to Wellington's Monument, just where Blackstone Edge meets Baslow Edge. Dr Wrench of Baslow had this monument erected in 1866 at his own expense at a place considered by G.H.B. Ward to have few equals – 'the elevation seems particularly suited for the graceful grouping of the scenery.' The vista extends right down the Derwent Valley over Chatsworth's head to Darley Dale and westwards beyond Buxton, to Axe Edge.

Easy walking along Curbar Edge.

A track now continues northwards, past the Eagle Stone, where young men from Baslow once used to demonstrate their prowess and preparedness for marriage by climbing the rock. It is just a gentle amble along the spine of Baslow Edge towards the impressive profile of Curbar Edge and the end of the walk.

INFORMATION
Start/Finish: Curbar Gap GR262747.
Distance/Time: 19km(12miles) / 6hours.
Grading: Moderate; on good paths, tracks and hill roads along gritstone edges and across exposed moorland.
Maps: OS Outdoor Leisure sheet 24 White Peak Area.
Refreshments: The Grouse Inn; Robin Hood Inn below Birchen Edge; Curbar Gap in season.
Public Transport: Trains from Sheffield and Manchester to Grindleford; buses to Baslow area from Chesterfield, Buxton and Bakewell.

The three 'battleship' tors at Birchen Edge.

Evening light on Curbar Edge.

Gardom's Edge.

WALK 17 Bretton Clough and Abney Moor

To the north of the village of Eyam is a broad stretch of folded moorland, its flanks deeply cut by the trenches of Bretton and Abney Cloughs and separated from the northern moors by the Hope Valley. This unusual arc of gritstone heather moorland, surrounded on three sides by typical limestone countryside, might lack the impressive crag scenery of the gritstone edges to the east, but we should be thankful for this incursion across the Derwent, for the coarse sandstone has produced a unique landscape.

Starting from the village of Eyam, a circular walk can be enjoyed through wonderfully contrasting scenery of wooded cloughs, green fields and barren, open moorland and visits the villages of Grindlow and Foolow. Eyam, usually referred to as 'the Plague Village' is a fascinating place and a rewarding day can be spent exploring its history.

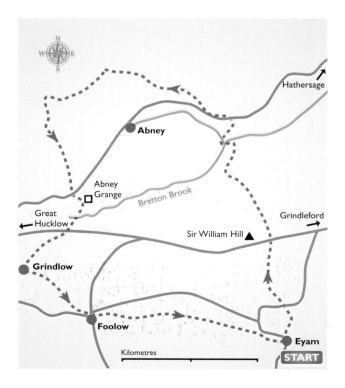

Walkers traversing the rim of Bretton Clough.

Eyam to Stoke Ford

From Eyam Town End the walk starts up the narrow lane climbing north out of the village, past the Miners Arms pub, by the appropriately-named Water Lane, whose series of water troughs and pipes were part of the local water supply established in 1588. A slanting ascent through fields then woodlands above Eyam youth hostel leads up to the breezy crest of Eyam Edge. Here you have a fine view back over Eyam to Middleton Dale, and the rolling plateau of the White Peak beyond, while in the southeast lies Chatsworth House in its wooded parkland.

Across the road a footpath is followed over Bole Hill, passing close to the old Ladywash lead mine, near the summit of the roughly-surfaced Sir William Hill Road. This famous road, originally the 1757 Sheffield to Buxton turnpike, is thought to have been named after Bess of Hardwick's grandson, Sir William Cavendish.

The rocky outcrop of Gotheredge above Bretton Clough, backed by the walled pastures on Abney Low.

Crossing Abney Moor.

Stoke Ford to Abney Grange

The path zigzags down to the small footbridge at Stoke Ford in a quiet, unspoilt wooded basin. Upstream from here, beyond a larch plantation, is the ancient village of Abney, meaning 'Abba's well-watered land', nestling in a hollow surrounded by high moorland.

After crossing the brook and climbing up to the Hathersage road, a track contours below Oaks Farm from where the slopes of Smelting Hill on the southern flanks of Offerton Moor are crossed on good, grassy paths. Swinging leftwards around the edge of the walled pastures Brough Lane is joined from where you have fine views up the Hope Valley to the shapely profile of Lose Hill. The lane is eventually quit for an obvious path that leads south across the sweep of Abney Moor to the road above Abney Grange, an ancient hamlet with monastic associations.

Our way lies north through heather across Eyam Moor from where a magnificent panorama opens up to the lofty Eastern Edges, from Stanage to Baslow, with Hathersage far below by the River Derwent. To the north-west, beyond Bretton Clough, is an intricate pattern of walled fields. Eyam Moor itself is a fascinating place with archaeological sites dating back to the middle centuries of the Bronze Age, the most significant being Wet Withens, a circle containing 16 blocks of gritstone surrounded by an earth bank. Smaller circles and several barrows are also found nearby.

Walled pastures between Foolow and Grindlow.

Crossing expansive heather moorland on the western flanks of Eyam Moor a good path descends gently to a curving grassy shelf over-looking bracken-covered slopes that sweep down into Bretton Clough. From a small rocky outcrop known as Gotheredge, set high above the clough, is an excellent view across the wooded valley to the walled pastures on Abney Low. Bretton Clough is now uninhabited but well into the nineteenth century moorland farming thrived here and the nearby ruined Gotheredge Farm was built in the seventeenth century. Also, according to local history, cattle were hidden in the clough from Prince Charlie's marauding Highlanders passing through Derbyshire in 1745 en route for London.

On the southwestern corner of Abney Moor lies Durham Edge, home of the Derbyshire and Lancashire Gliding Club. Here, on good days, you can see traditional gliders and modern, brightly-coloured hang gliders enjoying the thermals generated along the exposed Hucklow escarpment.

Abney Grange to Eyam

From Abney Grange, a path leads steeply down into the head of Bretton Clough, where complicated, shaley landslips can be seen on the south side of the valley. An equally steep ascent up the other side of the clough lands you at a narrow hill road hugging the crest of Hucklow Edge. On a clear day the broad tapestry to the southwest sweeps across the limestone plateau to the distant profile of Axe Edge, beyond Buxton.

Nestling below the wooded slopes to the southwest sits the village of Grindlow, approached along the narrow hill road then via a path across fields. On the southern end of the village a track, an old packhorse route in its early stages, leads past Roods Farm to the small village of Foolow. Formerly a lead mining village, this is a fascinating place complete with pub, seventeenth-century hall, village green and pond, besides which are a fourteenth-century cross and a stone block inset with an iron ring – thought to be a relic of bull-baiting which was outlawed in 1835.

A short way along the Eyam road, a path leads rightwards back to Eyam through a series of walled pastures, many linked by intricate, 'squeezer' stiles, skillfully hewn from gritstone which contrasts with the dry limestone walls.

Eyam's parish church of St Lawrence.

Eyam – the Plague Village

Originally a Saxon settlement, Eyam, with its beautiful church and seventh-century Saxon cross – one of the finest in the country – and well preserved old buildings, particularly the seventeenth-century Eyam Hall, home of the Wright family for over 300 years, has probably not changed much since the tragic event of 1665-66, when the Great Plague struck the village.

The Bubonic Plague, thought to have come from London in a box of clothes or fabric, decimated the village. A Plague Book in the parish church of St Lawrence lists the names of the victims, including the wife of the rector, William Mompesson. Led by Mompesson, the villagers quarantined themselves to prevent the disease spreading; an act of courage which probably cost more lives than in other locally afflicted towns and villages. Food and medical supplies were left at various points on the village boundary. Many touching memorials commemorating those who died are to be found on some cottages and in the surrounding fields, including the famous Riley Graves to the east of the village where a mother buried all her family. The annual plague commemoration service is held at nearby Cucklett Delf in late August to coincide with the well-dressing.

WALK 18 Seven Hathersage Halls

Tradition has it that Robert Eyre, who lived in the Hope Valley above Hathersage in the Middle Ages, installed each of his seven sons in dwellings that were in sight of one another and, by using coded signals, could keep in touch. A novel and interesting circular walk starting from Hathersage visits what are probably six of the seven halls, plus Highlow Hall, the most likely home of Robert Eyre himself.

Lying in a tributary valley leading down to the River Derwent, the popular village of Hathersage, had a thriving needle, pin and wire drawing industry in the nineteenth century. Although long gone, the old mill buildings still remain. The village looks up to St Michael's church, originating in the fourteenth and fifteenth centuries, and is associated with Little John, trusty lieutenant of Robin Hood. Inside the church are some lovely fifteenth- and sixteenth-century brasses of the Eyre family whose name was used in the novel, *Jane Eyre*. The author Charlotte Bronte stayed for three weeks with her friend Ellen Nussey at the vicarage, next to the church, in 1845 and it is thought that she based Morton, in *Jane Eyre*, on Hathersage.

Hathersage.

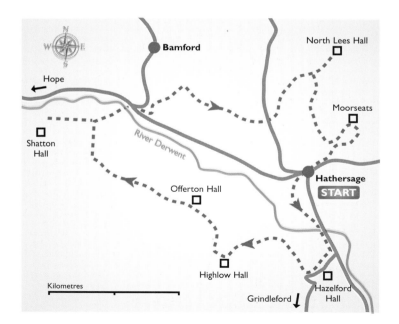

Hathersage to Shatton

On the southern outskirts of Hathersage, beyond the railway line, paths lead across fields to join the Grindleford road at Leadmill Bridge over the Derwent. Just beyond the hamlet of Leadmill, a lane leads up right towards the first hall, Hazelford Hall, with its gritstone ball finials and leaded lights. The lane is eventually left for a path leading right through pastures and across a stream before climbing up to the Broadhay Farm track, which leads to Abney Lane. About 800m/875yds left of here is the second hall, Highlow Hall, complete with ornate garden gateways and dovecote-like gazebo. It is certainly recorded that Robert Eyre, along with his 14 children, was living here in the latter part of the fifteenth century.

Hazelford Hall.

From Highlow Hall an ancient trackway leads northwest down through Dunge Wood before climbing up to Callow Farm and along to Offerton Hall, the next hall. Where the track enters Offerton Moor is the stone pillar of Robin Hood's Stoop from which place the outlaw is said to have shot an arrow for 2km/1.3miles into Hathersage churchyard – some shot! From Offerton Moor you can look northwest to Crookhill Farm above Ladybower Reservoir; one of the halls not visited on this walk. Offerton Hall with its ancient sheltering trees, cruck barn, and neighbouring Offerton House are soon reached. The moors behind this lonely settlement are crossed to join the old lane coming over the hill from Abney, and soon leads down to Shatton village, an attractive settlement of stone cottages and farms.

To see Shatton Hall, the fourth of the halls, requires an out-and-back detour over the nearby ford and along the sunken Townfield Lane until a view left across farmland allows a glimpse of the ancient hall.

Highlow Hall.

Shatton to North Lees Hall

Just beyond the ford at Shatton, on the left, is the Homestead at Nether Shatton, the fifth hall, whose original outbuildings a few yards down the lane have been converted into a modern house. The route now crosses the River Noe at Shatton Bridge just upstream of its confluence with the Derwent, and follows the A625 road right for a short distance in order to cross the Derwent at Mytham Bridge, and so along the road to Bamford railway station. Bamford, a former mill-village, just north of the station, clings to the slopes below the conspicuous Bamford Edge. Just beyond the station is Saltergate Lane, part of the old salt route between Cheshire and South Yorkshire, and leads right with fine views over Sickleholme Golf Course. At the top of the lane, at the entrance to the water Company's treatment plant, are the fine gateposts removed from Derwent Hall grounds before they were inundated by the waters of Ladybower Reservoir.

Our way is across the golf course up to Thorpe Farm, with its expansive vista south across the Derwent Valley to Offerton Moor and its pattern of ancient fields and barns which we passed earlier in the day. The farm track gives way to a narrow hill road that soon descends through deciduous woodland to the rear of Brookfield Manor, which bears a date of 1646 and is now an industrial training centre.

INFORMATION
Start/Finish: Hathersage.
Distance/Time: 19km(I2 miles) / 6hours.
Grading: Easy; along lanes and footpaths through pastureland and across open moors.
Maps: OS Outdoor Leisure sheet 1 Dark Peak Area and 24 White Peak Area.
Refreshments: Various pubs and Longlands Eating House in Hathersage; the Angler's Rest at Bamford.
Public Transport: Trains and buses from Manchester and Sheffield to Hathersage.

A short distance beyond Brookfield Manor and Bronte Cottage, a tarmac drive turns up to the left to North Lees Hall, its main tower visible from the lane. Located below Stanage Edge this is the sixth of the halls and perhaps the most fascinating architecturally. Standing on an ancient site the hall is a late-sixteenth-century tower house, more like a Border peel tower than a Peakland farmhouse. The celebrated Eyre family were tenants here from 1750 to 1882 and the building is thought to have been the original Thornfield Hall in *Jane Eyre*. Flanked by mature trees to the west and north, the hall, its surrounding estate and camp site, is now owned by the National Park Authority and farmed by Broomfield Agricultural College. The hall itself provides high-class holiday accommodation.

North Lees Hall to Hathersage

Heading back towards Brookfield Manor we follow a track through fields towards Hathersage. This valley of the Hood Brook is really domesticated parkland and very attractive for that, in contrast to the wilder slopes at Offerton above Shatton. A path presently forks up left towards the conspicuous spire of Hathersage church near where a path can be followed up the hill to lonely Moorseats. This last ancient hall, which may date from the Middle Ages, Charlotte Bronte modelled as the home of the Rivers family in *Jane Eyre*.

To reach Hathersage the walk takes the lane curving east to Carr Head Farm and continues along the track down to the church. Here yew trees shade the traditional grave of Little John and the clock chimes out through the tall trees to the old, hillside halls.

North Lees Hall.

WALK 19 Higger Tor and the Burbage Valley

The rocky outcrop of Higger Tor and the hill top fort of Carl Wark are two of the most prominent features overlooking the Burbage Valley and provide excellent vantage points for surveying the surrounding landscape, particularly northwest across the Derwent Valley to the moors of the Dark Peak. It is also an area with a fascinating historical background. As a contrast to these open moorlands dotted with numerous tors, this circular walk also visits the beautiful wooded Padley Gorge and the parkland grounds of the Longshaw estate. A good starting point is the parking area by the excellent café at Grindleford railway station at Upper Padley.

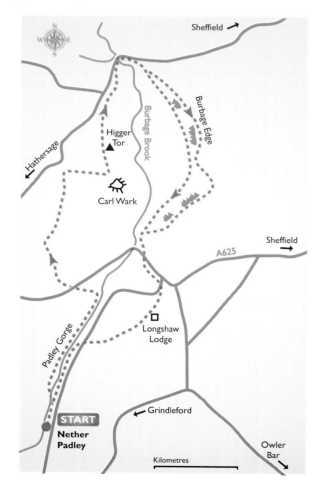

Burbage Brook tumbles through Padley Gorge.

Padley Gorge to Over Owler Tor

Although not on the actual itinerary, the nearby Padley Chapel, a short distance along the private road from the station, is well worth a visit. Restored in 1933 but dating from the fourteenth century, the chapel is famous for its association with the Padley Martyrs, who were executed during the Catholic persecutions in the reign of Elizabeth I. Each year in July a memorial service is held to commemorate the deaths of the two martyred priests.

Just beyond the café, past the gaping portal of Totley Tunnel on the right (the second longest in England) you enter the National Trust's secluded

Padley Gorge. This is an atmospheric sanctuary, rich in wildlife and whose steep, wooded slopes – remnants of ancient oak woodlands – look down on a stream that tumbles over a series of mossy boulders and cataracts. In autumn this is a magnificent place when the golden brown leaves of the oak and beech trees are a blaze of colour. A short distance into the wood, a footbridge crosses the stream from where the tree-cloaked left bank can be followed up to the open upper section of Burbage Brook and the A625 Hathersage road, opposite the car park.

Over Owler Tor to Burbage

Beyond the car park a stile gives access to a path that climbs the bouldery moor, past Mother Cap Tor up to the prominent rocky outcrop of Over Owler Tor. On a clear day you get a tremendous view up the Derwent Valley to the familiar cone-shaped Win Hill backed by the hills of the Dark Peak. Across Hathersage Moor to the east are our next objectives, the two flat-topped hills of Higger Tor and Carl Wark, which are reached along heathery tracks along the ridge top towards Winyards Nick then eastwards across Hathersage Moor.

As you approach Carl Wark it is easy to see why this naturally defensive site was chosen as a fort. Thought to date back to the Iron Age or before, this crude, enclosed plateau protected on three sides by steep, rocky slopes, has its northern rampart faced with large gritstone blocks. Although the actual date of Carl Wark is uncertain, it is certainly one of the area's outstanding hillforts and well worth a close inspection. From Carl Wark, beyond a marshy depression, a badly eroded track points the way up to the chaotic, rocky summit of Higger Tor with its huge, leaning block.

Burbage to Upper Padley

The edge path is now followed round below the Fiddler's Elbow Road to Upper Burbage Bridge and the start of Duke's Drive, a green lane leading down the Burbage Valley. An alternative to the green lane is to follow the more exposed path along the craggy eastern lip of the valley, from where you get an interesting perspective across the valley's woods and bracken-covered slopes to the rocky knolls of Higger Tor and Carl Wark. Eventually the natural edge merges with a quarried section from where a path joins the green drive at the road just below the Fox House Inn.

Across the road is the Longshaw Country Park with its splendid lodge built around 1830 for the Duke of Rutland. Good tracks lead south near the lodge, now owned by the National Trust, passing a lake, rhododendron bushes and tall conifers, eventually crossing the Grindleford road to re-enter the woods of Padley Gorge near the start of the walk.

INFORMATION
Start/Finish: Railway station at Upper Padley GR 250788.
Distance/Time: 12km(8miles) / 5hours.
Grading: Easy; along good moorland and woodland paths.
Maps: OS Outdoor Leisure sheet 24 White Peak Area and 1 Dark Peak Area.
Refreshments: Cafés at Upper Padley and Longshaw Lodge; the Fox House Inn near Burbage.
Public Transport: Served by trains from Sheffield and Manchester and buses from Bakewell, Chesterfield and Sheffield.

Walkers leaving Over Owler Tor for Carl Wark.

Burbage Edge.

The huge leaning block at Higger Tor.

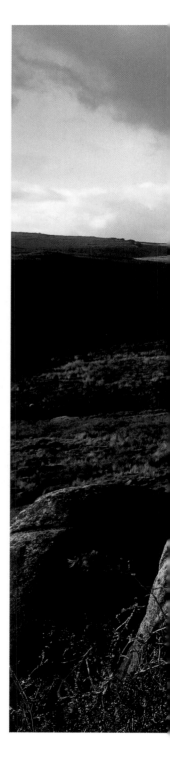

Carl Wark overlooking Burbage Valley.

WALK 20 Stanage Edge

High above the village of Hathersage sits the extensive gritstone escarpment of Stanage Edge from whose rocky crest the broad, heathery sweep of Hallam Moor dips eastwards towards the Rivelin Valley and Sheffield. The steep gritstone buttresses of the 6.5km/4miles long Stanage Edge were first explored in the late nineteenth century, and have provided challenges to generations of rock climbers. For many climbers, Stanage is Mecca; while for walkers, the views from this breezy and airy promenade are one of the great attractions, especially northwards to Win Hill and Lose Hill, and beyond, the wild heather moorland of the plateaux of Kinder and Bleaklow.

Lying in a tributary valley leading down to the River Derwent, the village of Hathersage is an excellent starting point for this walk. One of the

village's main industries was once based on grindstone making and during the walk numerous abandoned grindstones can be seen below Stanage Edge. The village is associated with Little John, trusty lieutenant of Robin Hood. After traversing Stanage Edge, this fascinating circular walk returns to Hathersage through pastureland and picturesque woods.

Hathersage to Crow Chin

Leaving the village near the post office, Baulk Lane is followed northwards to enter green pastures along a track from where you get tantalising glimpses of the distant buttresses on Stanage Edge. The track, which lies above the Hood Brook, passes Brookfield Manor to a country lane near the drive to North Lees Hall.

After walking up the drive, the castellated sixteenth-century building is passed on the right up some steps to gain a track across hillside pastures, leading to a small, charming plantation of mixed woodland. After ascending beside a stream through the trees you arrive at the old turnpike road which once linked Sheffield with Thornhill, on the slopes of Win Hill. Here, the full majesty of Stanage Edge is revealed, its continuous line of grey buttresses stretching away leftwards to the prows of High Neb and Crow Chin.

Across the road is open country, through which a path climbs up towards the edge, joining another path from nearby Hollin Bank car park to enter Stanage Plantation. A path, paved in places with gritstone slabs, rises up through the scattered pine trees. This is known as Jacob's Ladder and is probably an ancient trod for packhorses dating back to the eighteenth century. Whatever its history, the path provides an easy ascent as it slants up below the crags to arrive on the crest through a weakness in the escarpment rim. Pause here to take in the immediate views of the gritstone buttresses and the brilliant vista up the Derwent Valley beyond Bamford Moor to Kinder Scout while to the west is the heather-covered dome of Offerton Moors.

Heading northwards along the crest of the edge you meet the Long Causeway, a Roman Road and later a packhorse way, climbing up from the left on its way to Sheffield via Stanedge Pole, visible to the right across heather moorland. The edge is now quitted for a path that traverses the bracken-covered slopes below the crags, towards the obvious overhang of High Neb buttress.

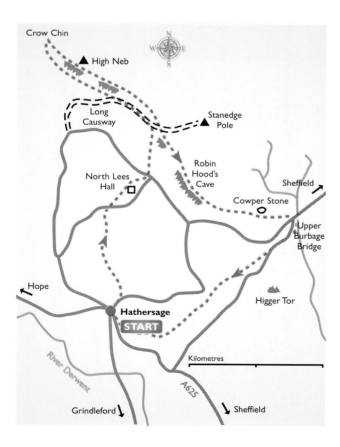

Looking northwest along Stanage Edge to High Neb.

Here, scattered on the slopes below High Neb are numerous discarded millstones, some stacked ready for transportation, while others are hidden by dense bracken. The finished stones would have been fitted with wooden axles and carted over the Long Causeway to the early water powered edge-tool works that occupied the wooded valleys. Many of High Neb's grindstones are finished with centre holes and some are partly worked, testimony to the sudden end of this important local industry. Imported finer stones and the invention of synthetic carborundum contributed to its downfall

Crow Chin to Burbage Brook

The path leads on to below Crow Chin, where the edge swings northwards by the remains of two ancient burial cairns towards Moscar. Stanage's crest is now regained up the bouldery slopes, just a short distance from the trig point on High Neb, at 458m/1502ft, the highest point on the escarpment and the highest within the city boundary of Sheffield, making it one of the most elevated large cities in Europe. From the Neb you can gaze out at the great panorama of higher Peakland with the long line of Kinder Scout as the central feature rearing up beyond Bamford Moor. To the left are the shapely peaks of Win Hill, Lose Hill and Mam Tor's weathered face with the distant uplands of the White Peak stretching to the southwest.

Keep your eyes peeled here for the small, numbered scoops cut into the tops of some of the buttresses by gamekeepers at the beginning of the nineteenth century. These were used to hold water or grit for the grouse that were reared for the shoots. Until relatively recent times much of these crags and moors were keepered and free access only became possible through agreements with the Peak Park and owners.

From High Neb the edge path can be followed southeastwards as it meanders along the tops of an almost continuous line of gritstone buttresses; one of Britain's premier climbing grounds. One of the features to look out for is Robin Hood's Cave, sited at the back of a balcony beneath the crest.

The path continues above diminishing crags to a bouldery summit capped by a triangulation point which is just one metre lower than High Neb. From here you get fine views ahead to Higger Tor and Burbage Edge. Leaving the summit behind, the moor is descended to the east, passing the impressive leaning Cowper Stone where in summer you might hear the chatter of ring ouzels, commonly known as mountain blackbirds. The path joins the Ringinglow Road just west of Upper Burbage Bridge at the head of the valley of Burbage Brook.

Millstones below High Neb.

Burbage Brook to Hathersage

From the bridge, the upper of two good paths heads southwards across heather slopes, traversing below Fiddler's Elbow, before dropping down to the narrow hill road from where a path traverses across Callow Bank into a walled lane leading down to Mitchell Field Farm. By continuing leftwards on a path through pastureland, you eventually pass Scraperlow, beyond which woodland leads down to join the main road just outside Hathersage.

> **INFORMATION**
> **Start/Finish:** Car park at Hathersage GR 231814.
> **Distance/Time:** 14km(9miles) / 4hours.
> **Grading:** An easy walk on field and moorland paths and along gritstone edges.
> **Maps:** OS Outdoor Leisure sheet 1 Dark Peak Area.
> **Refreshments:** Various pubs and Longlands Eating House in Hathersage.
> **Public Transport:** Served by buses from Sheffield and Bakewell and trains from Sheffield and Stockport.

Winter arrives below Stanage Edge. Win Hill in the distance backed by Kinder Scout and Bleaklow.

Far left: *Evening climbing on the buttresses at High Neb.*

Above left: *Robin Hood's Balcony Cave area, Stanage.*

Above: *Stanage, a Mecca for rock climbers.*

Left: *Numbered scoops cut into the rocks above Stanage provided water for grouse.*

WALK 21   Along the Derwent Crest

Derwent Edge, the most northerly of the Eastern Edges, looks down on the waters of Derwent and Ladybower Reservoirs far below. Unlike the other edges it has no really continuous section of gritstone buttresses, but a series of strange, wind-eroded tors sitting on the edge of the moor. It forms a splendid walk, especially when combined with a descent of the deeply-cut Abbey Clough.

The name Derwent comes from the Celtic word 'derwen' meaning oak, and Derwent Dale must have once been a beautiful wooded valley. Nowadays pine and larch plantations cover much of the lower slopes and the once peaceful dale is a popular tourist spot for visitors who come

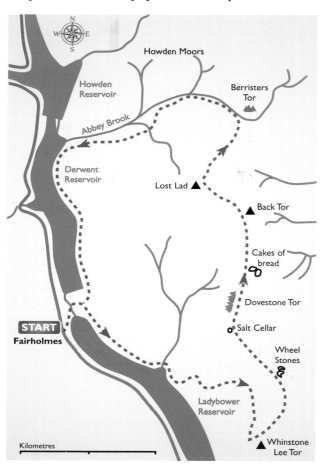

and marvel at the three dams that hold back the waters of the Derwent. The impressive Howden, Derwent and Ladybower Reservoirs are hemmed in between the Howden Moors in the east and the mighty bulk of Bleaklow in the west and the valley is often referred to as the Peak's Lake District.

Fairholmes to Back Tor

A good starting point for this walk is the Fairholmes visitor centre car park at the head of Ladybower Reservoir. A road leads down from Fairholmes crossing the bridge below the Derwent Dam wall which, during periods of heavy rainfall, creates a dramatic waterfall curtain. The road gives easy access to a bridleway that runs along the full length of all three reservoirs up to Slippery Stones at the head of the valley. The shoreline of Ladybower can now be followed, first along a metalled section to Wellhead Farm, just beyond which, at a small bridge, is the site of the hamlet of Derwent that was submerged when the valley was flooded.

The track is soon quitted up to the left through pastures, passing between two rustic barns and, beyond the Grindle Clough ford, a steady climb leads up to the start of Derwent Edge near Whinstone Lee Tor. Seen from here across Ladybower, Win Hill appears as a true peak, yet still dwarfed by the long, almost horizontal ridge of Kinder Scout which dips to the Snake Pass road. To the right, trenched valleys merge into the Bleaklow massif and the Howden Moors sweep over Margery Hill to the northern end of Derwent Edge.

Our route heads along the ridge, crossing the old packhorse route connecting Derwent with Moscar to the east. The conspicuous Wheel Stones, the first of the rocky outcrops, are visible ahead and are also known as the Coach and Horses. These are the first of many wind-eroded gritstone outcrops and pinnacles found along Derwent Edge, their intriguing names reflecting the appearance of the rocks. A particular favourite with photographers is the Salt Cellar, which appears on your left as you approach the buttresses of Dovestone Tor, a popular venue with rock climbers.

Beyond the steep cliffs the path continues north, passing the shapely Cakes of Bread and climbing to the conspicuous rounded rocks of Back Tor complete with a triangulation point cemented into the topmost

Approaching the Wheel Stones (or Coach and Horses) on Derwent Edge.

rocks. At 538m/1765ft, Back Tor is one of the best viewpoints on the walk, with tremendous moorland scenery, especially across to the summit plateau of Bleaklow.

In an attempt to reduce the erosion along the boggy sections of Derwent Edge, the National Trust have recently laid a stone-flagged pavement so route finding in this area is not a problem.

123

Lost Lad and Abbey Clough

A paved track now drops westwards to the cairned summit of Lost Lad, another fine vantage point with the toposcope erected by the famous Clarion Ramblers in memory of W.H. Baxby. The hill supposedly takes its name from a shepherd boy who was lost on the moors while gathering sheep one winter's day. A shepherd who discovered the words 'Lost Lad' scratched on a nearby rock eventually found the boy's body; a stark reminder of how unforgiving these hills can be under a mantle of snow and thick mist.

The paved path continues across open moorland to Lost Lad Hillend, from where you can descend northeastwards into Sheepfold Clough to the remains of a shooting cabin at the junction with Abbey Clough – the longest and finest side valley in the Derwent area. These upper reaches of the clough are very impressive, with fine views of waterfalls and rocky gorges.

Our way now heads down the south flank of Abbey Clough past a fascinating landslip below the prominent grey crag of Berristers Tor. Here you can really appreciate the sheer scale and majesty of this splendid clough. On the OS map this valley is shown as Howden Dean, a bit of a paradox since it is thought that Howden meant 'deep valley' and Dean also meant 'valley'. However, to walkers it is affectionately known as Abbey Clough.

Opposite the waterfalls in the strangely named Gravy Clough the valley opens up to give a beautiful view across Derwent Reservoir to Birchinlee Pasture. A path contours round the hillside, eventually passing through slopes scattered with oaks which lead down to the forestry track alongside Derwent Reservoir.

The valley of Abbey Brook takes its name from the former grange of Welbeck Abbey in Nottinghamshire, when in the thirteenth-century King John granted the upper Derwent Estate to the abbey and the area became an agricultural estate, centred on the old Derwent village. The daffodils at the entrance to Abbey Clough are said to have been planted by those medieval monks.

The gentle stroll back to Fairholmes along the wooded edge of Derwent Reservoir is a pleasant and relaxing way to end this walk.

Looking west from Whinstone Lee Tor across Ladybower Reservoir to Crook Hill.

INFORMATION
Start/Finish: Fairholmes car park GR 173893.
Distance/Time: 16km(10miles) / 6hours.
Grading: Difficult; a moorland walk along mainly good paths. Extra care needed in bad visibility and good navigation skills needed.
Maps: OS Outdoor Leisure sheet 1 Dark Peak Area and Harveys Superwalker Dark Peak.
Refreshments: Fairholmes; the Ladybower Inn and Yorkshire Bridge Inn near Bamford.
Public Transport: Railway station at Bamford. Upper Derwent Valley served by buses from Sheffield and Glossop. A minibus runs along the valley at weekends.

Derwent Edge overlooking Ladybower Reservoir.

Far left: *The Salt Cellar, Derwent Edge.*

Left: *Sunset from Back Tor, Derwent Edge.*

Below left: *Walkers approaching Lost Lad.*

Below: *The dramatic landslip in Abbey Clough.*

127

Bradfield Moors and Back Tor

High and Low Bradfield.

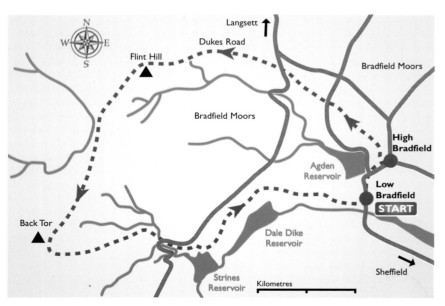

B radfield Dale, to the northwest of Sheffield, is one of the least-known major valleys in the Peak District. In the upper section its western flanks are cloaked in dense woods which open up to heather moorland rising gently to the summit ridge of Derwent Edge separating Bradfield Dale from the popular Derwent Valley with its reservoirs. Bradfield Dale also has its own catchment dams which are seen from the Moscar to Langsett road, one of the most scenic hill roads in the Dark Peak, and are visited during this circular walk after crossing the wild Bradfield Moors.

The walk starts from the village of Low Bradfield with its scattering of houses and farm buildings in a lovely valley setting, overlooked on three sides by hills and sitting alongside the confluence of the Agden Dike and Dale Dike. Above the village perches High Bradfield with its Norman church, the first objective on the walk.

Low Bradfield to the Derwent Watershed

From Kirk Bridge, just below Agden dam wall, a path climbs uphill towards High Bradfield from where you get lovely views over the moors to Derwent Edge. High Bradfield's towered St Nicholas's church, of Norman origin, retains its former watch house, built in 1754 to deter body snatchers.

Beyond the churchyard a path contours round to a wood and the nearby tree covered Bailey Hill, site of a Norman motte and bailey earthwork. After a steep descent through gloomy conifers, Roche End Brook is crossed, and the fields traversed below the impressive crumbling grit-stone cliffs of neglected Agden Rocher, once popular with Sheffield climbers. The path continues past the ruins of Rocher Head where a rough lane leads up to a minor road beyond which a path runs parallel to a lane across semi-moorland. Just west of here is Mortimer House – named to honour Hans Winthrop, Lord of the Manor of Bamford, who promoted a Road Act in 1711 to build the Thornhill to Penistone hill road, which lost him money.

Our path soon reaches this road where it cuts through the 412m/1350ft long ancient Bar Dyke, an entrenchment thought to date back to the Iron Age or Dark Ages. The Duke of Norfolk's Road – so named because this moorland came into the Duke's estates under an Enclosure Act of 1811 – is followed west, giving a gentle way up towards the Derwent watershed. This was once called 'the loneliest, wildest walk in South Yorkshire' but, especially in the first couple of kilometres, it is an easy track. The tower of Emley Moor television transmitter can be seen 19km/12miles to the north. Notice too, the occasional stone marking the boundary of the Broomhead Moors, which were once the most productive grouse country in Britain.

Derwent Watershed to Strines Bridge

The path eventually deteriorates and turns south from Flint Hill across boggy terrain which, in misty conditions or under a mantle of snow, can require careful navigation, especially over Cartledge Flat. Avoid the temptation to swing down towards the narrowing head of Abbey Brook and instead follow a sponge-like peaty path, keeping to the highest ground along Cartledge Stones Ridge up to the rocks around Back Tor, at 538m/1765ft, the highest point on the walk.

These eroded boulders and tors provide one of the best viewpoints in the Dark Peak, giving wide vistas to every point of the compass. John Derry, writing in his 1926 classic *Across the Derbyshire Moors*, considered the place 'a fitting region for creatures who love loneliness' and where 'the spirit of the moors has his throne on Back Tor. Also it does one good to get up into this upland, age-long solitude, where the primeval world is felt to be a mighty fact, linked to us'. Looking from here across to Mam Tor and the Great Ridge, Kinder Scout and the huge expanse of Bleaklow beyond Derwent Dale, many walkers will agree with Derry.

Just south of Back Tor, along a slabbed path, is Bradfield Gate Head, where the walk turns left down the gentle moor-side towards Foulstone Dyke. All this eastern dip slope was decoy country in the last war, with lights set up to attract German bombs away from Sheffield. The path goes down below the keeper's cottage at Foulstone Delf before entering the different world of coniferous plantations and to Strines Bridge and the lovely, narrow Moscar-Langsett hill road. The Strines Inn, a short distance right along the road towards Moscar, makes a good break in the walk.

Top right: *Boot's Folly*.

Right: *Bents House and Strines Reservoir backed by Brogging Moss.*

Strines Bridge to Low Bradfield

The walk now takes on yet a different character as it heads north along the road, taking the first track down to the right towards Strines Reservoir, passing Brogging Farm, and on by Stubbing Farm to ancient Hallfield, once part of the Fitzwilliam Estates. This old yeoman farm with its cruck barn, looks over Dale Dike Reservoir and back up Bradfield Dale to the conspicuous Boot's Folly, a stone look-out tower erected in 1927 by the Sheffield building contractor Charles Boot of nearby Sugworth Hall, built to find work for unemployed local men. The bridleway circumnavigates Hallfield and its buildings and we soon reach Dale Road beyond Thompson House Farm.

This quiet, minor hill road leads downhill and just after turning sharp right across the Annet Bridge over Dale Dike, a footpath leads east along the banks of the stream to a walled lane which re-enters Low Bradfield.

The Great Sheffield Flood

The Sheffield Water Authority turned its attention to Bradfield Dale in the middle of the nineteenth century and the Dale Dike reservoir was completed in the winter of 1863-64 just upstream from the village of Low Bradfield. It held 700 million cubic feet of water with a surface area of 78 acres/32hectacres. Heavy rain, driven by a gale, occurred on the 11 March 1864, testing the new impounding wall to such an extent that a crack appeared in it that evening. By midnight the wall had given way and it was reported that the flood 'swept like an avalanche down the course of the River Loxley to Hillsborough, and down the Don through the town, deluging the valley on both sides to a depth of many feet'.

More than 4500 homes were flooded, destroying 39 of them and 240 people were killed, making this one of the biggest ever single peacetime disasters in Britain. A replacement dam was completed in 1875 just upstream of the original one, the site of the latter now hidden by a coniferous plantation.

INFORMATION
Start/Finish: Low Bradfield. GR 263920.
Distance/Time: 21km(13miles) / 6hours.
Grading: Very difficult; a high level moorland walk but also includes easy walking along good paths, tracks and narrow hill roads through pastureland. In bad visibility good navigation skills are needed on the Derwent watershed section.
Maps: OS Outdoor Leisure sheet 1 Dark Peak Area and Harveys Superwalker Dark Peak.
Refreshments: Strines Inn and the Plough at Low Bradfield.
Public Transport: Buses from Sheffield to Low Bradfield.

Approaching Back Tor across the moors of Cartledge Flat.

Eroded rocks at Back Tor.

KINDER SCOUT AREA

Kinder Scout is a wilderness of heather, oozing black peat hags, deep drainage channels (known as groughs), and stark eroded gritstone outcrops and boulders. At 636m/2088ft, the undulating plateau is the Peak District's highest point and attracts walkers from the surrounding conurbations of Manchester, Sheffield and the Midlands. Kinder Scout sheds much of its water over a craggy ravine towards Hayfield to produce an impressive waterfall and it is thought that the modern name of Kinder Scout may be from a Norse one, meaning 'Hill of the Waterfall'. These botanically important Dark Peak moors are also among the few remaining examples of blanket bog in Europe.

Historically, Kinder Scout has played a major role in access to open moorlands culminating in the famous 1932 mass trespass involving the late Benny Rothman and his 400 companions, who set off from the quarry at Bowden Bridge car park east of Hayfield, an event commemorated by a plaque set into a gritstone buttress. The ramblers were furious that they were not allowed on Kinder's high plateau that was strictly preserved by the landowners for grouse shooting. It was as the group ascended William Clough that they had their famous confrontation with the gamekeepers on the grassy slopes below Sandy Heys, as a result of which five of the protesters received prison sentences. Sadly, Benny Rothman died early in 2002.

The event helped pave the way for the formation of National Parks fifty years ago. Kinder Scout is now owned and protected by the National Trust.

Kinder's size is very deceptive. Only 13square km/5square miles of plateau, its rugged northern slopes are connected to Bleaklow by the narrow neck of Featherbed Moss, while the Woodlands Valley, through which the Snake road passes, acts as a natural boundary between the two. To the south, gentle slopes lead from Kinder around the Vale of Edale to the ridge linking Rushup Edge, Mam Tor and Lose Hill.

Between these boundaries, solitude can still be found but the plateau can be punishing to the careless. Its weather can be unpredictable, and Kinder's top is very oppressive under a thick cloud, calling for accurate map and compass work and has ended the aspirations of many a Pennine Wayfarer. In dry weather the dusty peat can look like desert sand dunes, while in heavy rain it becomes black and slimy. In summer the moors are clothed in heather, cloudberry and cotton grass and the air is alive to the calls of golden plover ('the watchman of the moors'), curlews, red grouse and skylarks. But go there on a cold frosty morning in February when the peat hags are frozen hard, with the sun shining down from a clear blue sky and you will find the walking on Kinder at its most magnificent.

With a deep covering of snow – a rare occurrence these days – the plateau can become the domain of Langlauf (cross-country) skiers and when the Downfall freezes to a curtain of ice, mountaineers, armed with axes and crampons, queue up to tackle the steep face. In dry weather the gritstone outcrops dotted around Kinder's perimeter attract rock climbers. Whatever the weather, Kinder Scout is a very special place.

A perfect winter's day on Kinder Scout.

WALK 23   Mam Tor and the Great Ridge

Mam Tor dominates the undulating ridge which stretches from Lord's Seat, an ancient burial mound on Rushup Edge, to Lose Hill, passing through some of the most spectacular scenery in the area. This popular ridge, simply known as the Great Ridge, acts as a boundary between the dark Kinder grits and shales to the north and the white limestone scenery to the south.

The amazing geological features of this area make the surrounding countryside very popular with walkers, and an entertaining circular trip can be followed from Castleton at the head of the Hope Valley. Castleton is an excellent example of a medieval village and is surrounded on three sides by splendid hills whose rocks are riddled with fine show caves and old mines.

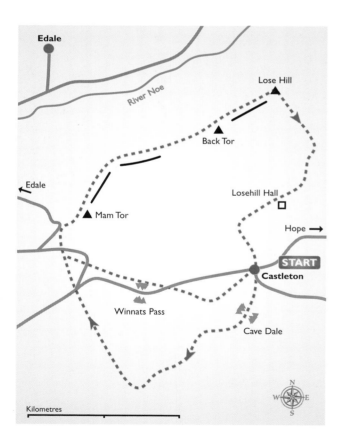

Described in 1683 by Thomas Hobbes as one of the seven Wonders of the Peak, Peak Cavern is a must and its approach along a deep gorge must be one of the most magnificent cave entrances in Britain. It was known in ancient times as the 'Devil's Arse', a name recently re-instated. The place has a fascinating history and for over 400 years a group of rope makers lived in a small village just inside the cave. The Normans built a castle on a very defensive rocky ridge above the cave ravine and Cave Dale, and the ruins of this once impressive fortification, identified with William Peveril, William of Normandy's son, still stand.

Cave Dale to Mam Tor

Our route starts from the village centre and takes the concealed entrance into the narrow defile of Cave Dale. Starting as a gentle, grassy-bottomed dry dale, it soon closes in at a rocky gorge then leads up onto open pastureland, where relics of abandoned lead mines are apparent around Dirtlow Rake. As you head right along Rowter Lane, a fine view of Mam Tor dominates the skyline ahead, and after crossing the B6061 you arrive at Windy Knoll, at the head of the Winnats Pass.

Winnats (meaning 'wind gates') is an impressive rocky pass through reef limestone down which a steep road leads to Castleton. An alternative start to the circuit is to ascend the pass or, better still, follow the grassy summit ridge over Treak Cliff on the northern flanks of the gorge. From the rim path you can look down on several impressive limestone ridges – Elbow Ridge and the aptly named Matterhorn Ridge. Treak Cliff is famous for its deposits of Blue John, a semi-precious banded fluorspar which has been worked for centuries to produce spectacular pieces, some of which are to be found in Chatsworth House.

Beyond Windy Knoll Cave, where bones of brown bear, wolf and hyena were excavated, the B6061 road is crossed to a car park below Mam Nick, through which the narrow hill road to Edale passes. Mam Tor (517m/1695ft), now owned by the National Trust, is ascended up a constructed path to the OS column at the paved summit. Despite its popularity the top is still an impressive place, a place to linger for a while and admire the views, especially across the Edale Valley to Kinder Scout.

Cave Dale is overlooked by Peveril Castle.

The steep northeast face of Back Tor.

Looking across the crumbling face of Mam Tor
(the Shivering Mountain) to Lose Hill.

It is Mam Tor's crumbling east face which gives rise to the name 'Shivering Mountain', and which has been responsible for the dune-like pastures on its lower slopes. The hill is still unstable as the broken sections of Telford's turnpike road below the face testify. Mam Tor's hill fort, the largest in the Peak District, supposedly overlaps the Bronze and Iron Ages. There is no better defensive position in the area and it is worth exploring the well-preserved double trench enclosing about 16acres/6.5ha of the summit.

Along the Great Ridge

From Mam Tor the ridge sweeps round in a graceful curve towards craggy Back Tor, its disintegrating northwest face mirroring that of Mam Tor. Between the two hills, the ridge dips to the memorial topograph at Hollins Cross. Before the church was built at Edale (it was consecrated in 1633), the pass was the high point on the 'coffin route' from Edale to Castleton church. Continuing along the ridge, an eroded slope leads steeply up Back Tor, whose craggy profile gives the Great Ridge such distinction when seen from Kinder Scout – especially in winter. To reduce the erosion along this section, the National Trust has paved much of the ridge path.

From the few remaining trees at the top of Back Tor it is only a short distance to Lose Hill (476m/1563ft), its upper slopes known as Ward's Piece. On a summer's evening the summit of Lose Hill is a lovely spot to rest and enjoy the views across the Edale valley to Win Hill with the silvery trail of the River Noe meandering below its southern slopes. It's all downhill now on good, though steep tracks southwards to Losehill Hall, the National Park Study Centre, from where a path leads from behind the hall back to the fleshpots of Castleton.

INFORMATION
Start/Finish: Castleton.
Distance/Time: 12km(7.5miles) / 4hours.
Grading: Easy; on good paths and tracks with a few steep ascents.
Maps: OS Outdoor Leisure sheet 1 Dark Peak Area and Harveys Superwalker Dark Peak.
Refreshments: Various pubs and teashops in Castleton.
Public Transport: Trains from Manchester and Sheffield to Hope. Buses to Castleton from Chesterfield, Sheffield and Manchester.

A group ascent of a snowy Mam Tor.

Crossing the Great Ridge towards Back Tor.

Winnats Pass and its rocky ridges.

Ward's Piece

G.H.B. Ward (1876–1957), the pioneer 'King of Ramblers', founded the Sheffield Clarion Ramblers in 1900, claimed as the first active working-class rambling club in Britain. He believed passionately in the right of ordinary folk to explore the health-giving uplands on foot, and came to be hated by gamekeepers and many landowners. In 1926 Ward founded the Sheffield and District Federation of the Ramblers' Association and was instrumental in the formation of the Sheffield and Peak District Branch of the CPRE.

Two thousand walkers joined Ward on the summit of Lose Hill on a fine April day in 1945 to see him being handed the deeds of 54acres/22ha of that hill's summit in appreciation of his life's work, ever since called Ward's Piece. In his speech of thanks he claimed to have at last 'joined the gaffers' against whom he had waged war for so long to gain public access to the hills. At the same ceremony he in turn presented the deeds to the National Trust. A stone viewing pillar dedicated to Ward now marks the summit of Lose Hill.

The view from Lose Hill across the Vale of Edale to Kinder Scout.

137

WALK 24 Win Hill and Alport Castles

Sitting high above Ladybower Reservoir, wedge-shaped Win Hill has been popular with walkers for many years. Its familiar profile is visible from great distances and it was a favourite with Ebenezer Elliot, the famous nineteenth-century Sheffield Corn Law Rhymer who referred to it as 'a real mountain – King of the Peak!' Who would disagree, for the panoramic vista from its crested summit is arguably the finest in the area.

An ascent of Win Hill forms the high point at the start of this circular walk, crossing the Woodlands Valley into Alport Dale to visit Alport Castles, one of the biggest landslips in Britain, finally returning over high pastureland, to Ashopton Viaduct near the starting point at Ladybower's dam wall. Throughout the walk the views are superb.

Ladybower to the Woodlands Valley

From the car park at Heatherdene alongside Ladybower Reservoir, a path contours along the hillside before descending steps opposite the

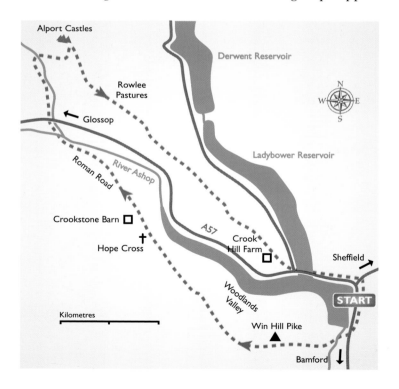

dam. After crossing the road a path leads steeply down past the grassy retaining wall of the reservoir and across Yorkshire Bridge to join a surfaced track. This is the route of the former narrow gauge railway used to carry rock for the construction of Howden and Derwent Reservoirs early last century. Just along the track to the right is Parkin Clough up which a stepped path, one of the steepest in the Peak District, climbs up alongside the clough below a canopy of conifers to delightful open moorland and the summit rocks of Win Hill Pike (462m/1518ft). Despite being at the end of a long spur sweeping down from Kinder Scout, the peak still retains its aloofness. From the craggy hill top the range of views are superb especially north across the two arms of Ladybower reservoir to the deeply seamed bulk of Bleaklow and the tor-pimpled Derwent Edge to its right.

The walk now follows the broad ridge towards Wooler Knoll, eventually joining the track coming up from the left. This road was thought to have been used by Roman legions as a link between the forts at Navio (Brough) and Melandra (Glossop) over the Snake Pass summit. At Hope Cross, a guidestone marking the crossing point of two old packhorse ways, the Roman road contours around the smooth, grassy eastern flanks of Kinder before descending to the confluence of the Rivers Ashop and Alport at the bridge opposite the entrance to Alport Dale. This deeply cut trench of Alport Dale is one of the most scenic approaches to the Bleaklow massif, especially if a faint riverside path is followed up to Grains-in-the-Water. The upper section of the valley also contains some of the loveliest waterfalls in the Peak District.

Woodlands Valley to Alport Castles

From Alport Bridge a path climbs through scrubby woodland to the access track for Alport Castles Farm. Here each July a strange ceremony known as the 'Love Feast' is held in a barn involving prayer and the taking of cakes and water. This historical tradition dates back to the seventeenth century, when the building was used as a retreat for Nonconformist services after they were made illegal by Charles II in 1662, when anyone of a Protestant persuasion was persecuted. John Wesley is said to have preached here.

The enormous landslip of Alport Castles.

The hillsides above and around the farms in lower Alport Dale have great swathes of conifer plantations, planted between 1920 and 1982 when there was a market for the timber. In 1994, the Forestry Commission planned to fell the trees and replace them with broad-leaf trees, but the building of a new road to carry the heavy machinery needed would have destroyed the valley. Fortunately the National Trust has recently bought the valley from the Forestry Commission and Severn Trent Water, incorporating it into its High Peak Estate. Over the next forty years, the National Trust will slowly replace the 426acres/172ha of conifers with oak, birch, rowan, holly, aspen and hazel, allowing the native wildlife to prosper.

By following a path bypassing the farm to the right, crossing a bridge spanning the River Alport, and then continuing up the steep grassy slopes, you arrive at the valley rim and the shattered rocks of Alport Castles, named after its resemblance to a crumbling medieval fortress. The Tower and its tiny plateau, known as Little Moor, have slipped away below the cliff face of Birchin Hat, where striated bands of grit-stone and shale have left a very unstable cliff and you may actually see pieces of rock falling to join the boulder slope below.

Looking north from the summit of Win Hill Pike across Ladybower Reservoir to Derwent Edge.

Alport Castles to Ladybower

We now turn southeast, across the grassy slopes of Rowlee Pasture. This attractive section is really an extension of the long spur which comes down from Bleaklow between the valleys of Westend and Alport and gives gentle walking on good paths, much of it alongside the western edge of Hagg Side woodlands overlooking Ladybower Reservoir. Beyond the woods an ascent over grassland leads to the unnamed summit of Bridge End Pasture from where you can follow a well-marked bridleway down past the two rocky humps of Crook Hill. The views from this section of the walk are splendid, especially west to the wooded Ashop Valley and Kinder Scout and to the craggy profile of Derwent Edge across the waters of Ladybower Reservoir.

Crookhill Farm is soon reached from where a path leads down fields to the Derwent Valley road a short distance from Ashopton Viaduct. A stroll alongside the road round the southeastern edge of Ladybower Reservoir soon brings us to Heatherdene car park and the end of the walk.

INFORMATION
Start/Finish: Heatherdene car park GR 202858.
Distance/Time: 20km(12.5miles) / 6hours.
Grading: Difficult; along good footpaths and tracks with several steep ascents.
Maps: OS Outdoor Leisure sheet 1 Dark Peak Area and Harveys Superwalker Dark Peak.
Refreshments: The Ladybower Inn on the A57, Yorkshire Bridge Inn just south of the start.
Public Transport: Railway station at nearby Bamford; buses from Sheffield and Manchester.

The Woodlands Valley.

WALK 25   Around Kinder Scout

Kinder Scout (636m/2088ft) the flattest, yet highest hill in the Peak District, has no real summit, and few visitors seek out its top although walkers in search of solitude, or wanting some practice with map and compass, can easily find it. E.A. Baker, author of *Moors, Crags and Caves of the High Peak*, at the beginning of last century, wrote that 'Kinder Scout offers solitude and established stillness older than the world'. However, for many, Kinder's greatest attractions lie around its perimeter where you find the best views and most dramatic rock architecture in the district.

The vast amphitheatre enclosing Kinder Downfall is the highlight of this walk around Kinder Scout's rim and is visited near the end of the walk when it is seen at its best in afternoon sunshine. For convenience the western approach from Bowden Bridge car park on the edge of Hayfield is used, although the circuit can be done just as easily from Edale. This is a challenging, high moorland trip and one that should not be underestimated, especially as conditions can change dramatically, and under a mantle of snow the outing can quickly become a major expedition. However, it is one of the classic walks of the Peak District with changing views around every corner.

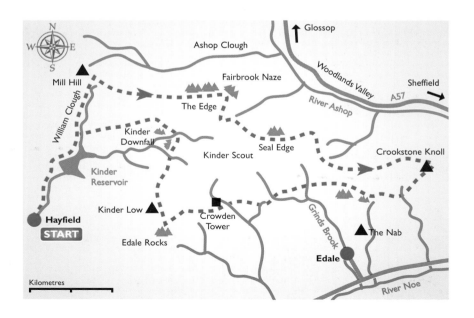

Hayfield to Ashop Head

The bustling little town of Hayfield, its wealth based on wool, cotton, paper and printing calico, was once a staging post on various packhorse routes across Kinder Scout. Now the village is a starting point for walkers approaching Kinder from the west. Hayfield's Packhorse public house – the last refreshment house for the jaggers crossing Kinder – is a reminder of those bygone days.

In its early stages the walk uses the route up William Clough taken by Benny Rothman and his companions in the famous 1932 Kinder mass trespass. The day starts from Bowden Bridge, along the Kinder Road towards the treatment plant buildings for Kinder Reservoir. Here, a cobbled bridleway climbs left of the buildings on to White Brow, from where you get a tantalising view across the reservoir towards the deep cleft of the Downfall ravine. The path makes a gradual descent across the lower bracken-covered slopes of Nab Brow overlooking the reservoir to the entrance of William Clough.

The path criss-crosses the stream in the steep clough up to the crossroads of paths below Ashop Head, which rises steeply on your right up to the Kinder plateau edge path. At Ashop Head the Pennine Way is met and here you can see the problems of erosion, and how careful restoration using natural gritstone has helped to slow the process.

Ashop Head to Grindsbrook

The first part of this high level walk goes left along The Edge, Kinder's northern escarpment of remote and windswept gritstone crags overlooking Ashop Clough, beyond which lies the broad plateau of Bleaklow. Along here you are often accompanied by the explosive, whirring sound of disturbed red grouse as they take flight.

Beyond the famous Boxing Glove Stones is the striking prow of Fairbrook Naze, where the path swings south around the head of Fairbrook Clough – a good escape route down to the Snake Inn in bad weather– then continues along the plateau rim past the outcrop of Chinese Wall on Seal Edge. Under a covering of snow, the aptly-named Seal Stones, overlooking Blackden Clough, look quite at home.

The Boxing Glove Stones on Kinder's northern edge.

Once past the head of the deeply-cut Blackden Clough – an excellent scrambling approach onto Kinder – the plateau slowly loses height to Crookstone Knoll at the end of a long spur, and the most easterly point on the walk. From this spot you can look northwards up the deep trench of Alport Dale to Bleaklow. Almost retracing your steps, the way ahead is now westwards, past the Mad Woman's Stones at the top of Jagger's Clough with its bracken-covered slopes. The eroded edge path, boggy in places, traverses above the narrow spine of Ringing Roger and along the rocky edges of Upper Tor and Nether Tor to Grindsbrook above Edale. All along this section you enjoy great views across to the Great Ridge from Lose Hill to Mam Tor.

Grindsbrook to Kinder Downfall

Contouring round the conical hill of Grindslow Knoll, the rocky outcrop of Crowden Tower, overlooking the craggy depths of Crowden Clough, is reached, and a fine vantage point to appreciate the vast summit plateau. Just west of Crowden Tower is a jumbled mass of weathered boulders and pinnacles known as the Woolpacks. A peaty path weaves a way around the boulders passing the prominent outcrops of Pym Chair and the wind-eroded towers of the aptly-named Pagoda. The walk westwards along a partly paved path through heather and peat to the anvil-shaped Noe Stool is a delight. A good edge path now swings around Edale Head, towards the sharp profile of Swine's Back, before turning northwards by Edale Rocks to join the Pennine Way at Kinder Low.

Through waves of brown peat, the route eventually crosses Red Brook before arriving at the Downfall ravine with its waterfall and spectacular crags of Kinder Great Buttress that, for rock climbers, must occupy one of the most exposed positions in the area. This ravine is Kinder's most precious gem and the high point of the walk.

In dry summers you might be disappointed by just a trickle of water running down the line of the waterfall, but not so during heavy rain when the place oozes atmosphere. And when gale force winds come from the southwest a huge wall of spray is blown back onto the plateau – quite an impressive sight and visible for miles. By contrast, in a hard winter the waterfall freezes to form a great, hanging curtain of translucent green and blue ice that offers some of the steepest snow and ice climbing in the Peak District. You can also look across the ravine down to the tiny Mermaid's Pool, resting on a grass shelf below a boulder-strewn slope. Legend has it that if you see the water nymph during Easter weekend you are granted immortality!

Walkers crossing towards Swine's Back from Noe Stool.

The Downfall to Hayfield

The River Kinder has cut a shallow furrow into the rocks and the path descends to cross it well back from the edge. Once across the river the edge path continues its way between gritstone rocks, to the eroded boulders at Sandy Heys from where you get a bird's-eye-view of Kinder Reservoir, and beyond, across the rounded hills to the serrated skylines of Stockport and Manchester. From Sandy Heys a faint path leads down steep, but easy grassy slopes to the bottom of William Clough where the outward route is rejoined back to Bowden Bridge.

On Kinder's northern edge.

INFORMATION
Start/Finish: Bowden Bridge car park on eastern edge of Hayfield GR: 048869; if full, park in Hayfield.
Distance/Time: 27km(17miles) / 7hours.
Grading: Very difficult; along moorland paths. Can be demanding in heavy rain, low cloud and deep snow. Experience in map and compass work essential.
Maps: OS Outdoor Leisure sheet 1 Dark Peak Area and Harveys Superwalker Dark Peak.
Refreshments: Pubs and cafés in Hayfield; drinks kiosk at Bowden Bridge car park.
Public Transport: Buses from Buxton, Glossop and Stockport.

The Moat Stone.

Above: *Ice-climbing in the Downfall ravine.*

Left: *The 'blow-back' at Kinder Downfall during strong southwesterly winds.*

Right: *Kinder Downfall – a frozen curtain.*

Far right: *In contrast Kinder Downfall is often only a trickle in summer.*

WALK 26 Chinley Churn and the Vale of Edale

To the southwest of the high gritstone moors of Kinder Scout, lies Chinley, an Old English name meaning 'clearing in the deep valley'. For many years Chinley, with its good rail links to Manchester and Sheffield, has been a popular starting point for walkers approaching Kinder Scout from the west.

Rising to the north of Chinley, between the Goyt and Sett valleys, is the shapely hill of Chinley Churn, a classic-shaped escarpment tilting up to the east, which has been extensively quarried in the past to produce paving stones and roof slabs. A fine network of tracks and paths now winds through the quarry leading up to the edge of the escarpment known as Cracken Edge.

Starting from Chinley, this walk traverses Cracken Edge, then follows the line of an ancient packhorse route across the flanks of Kinder Scout into the Vale of Edale, where the walk can be ended, returning by train from Edale. Alternatively, a longer circuit can be made across the tops of Brown Knoll, Mount Famine and South Head, with the final stage to Chinley being through secluded walled hill pastures.

Chinley to Chinley Head

From Station Road, the bridge to the war memorial is crossed and Maynestone Road followed right to where a path leads left between two houses. The faint path climbs steeply through fields towards the broken cliffs of Cracken Edge, crossing gorse-clad slopes up to a rough-surfaced walled lane. Another path, just along the lane to the right, now leads left between two farmhouses and climbs up to the lower edge of the quarries. A quarry track zigzags up the slopes before heading north beneath the cliffs where a steep rocky breach leads to the quarry rim.

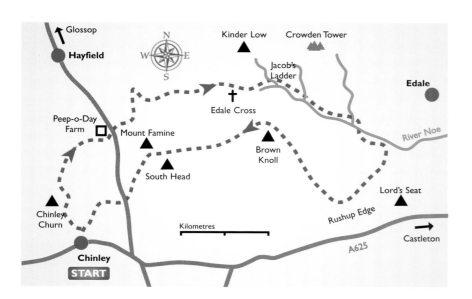

Above: *Coldwell Clough and Kinder Low End*

Left: *Looking southwest towards Chinley from the flanks of South Head.*

South Head seen from Mount Famine.

Although the quarrymen have long since gone, the shadows of their presence still remain, but Nature is slowly claiming back the boulder slopes while the disused lifting gear rusts away below the quarry rim.

The path soon dips down to join a grassy track that contours beneath further quarrying above some hawthorn woodland and winds down across pastureland, passing the solitary, semi-derelict house of Whiterakes, a typical hill holding, before joining the Hills Farm access road. The rough track descends right to a tarmaced lane by the house at Chinley Head. Built in 1841 and sitting astride the watershed between Hayfield and Chinley, the house, called Peep O'Day Farm faces east and has an unusual eye-shaped window over the door to catch the first rays of the early morning sunshine.

Chinley Head to Edale Cross

On the opposite side of the busy A624 road towards Hayfield, a lane beside a house leads up past an old quarry to join another rough, walled lane where a gate gives access to the neglected hill pastures on the northern shoulder of Mount Famine. As you pass through another gate at a dip on the skyline ahead you get a sudden view down into the deep Sett Valley at Coldwell Clough, with the frowning heights of Kinder Scout beyond.

From the gate, a steep descent down a rutted bridleway takes you to a lane which climbs right up to delightful Coldwell Clough Farm with its numerous gritstone carvings, including that of a flowering plant over an outhouse door. The road ends at the last of the trees and an old track continues up to Edale Cross set in its little enclosure at 533m/1750ft above sea level at a col between Brown Knoll and Swine's Back. This medieval marker stone lies on the packhorse trail connecting Edale with Hayfield and was also known as the Monk's Road. The stone's purpose is uncertain but it may have been used to mark the boundary of the lands owned by Basingwerk Abbey in Flintshire as early as the twelfth century.

Jacob's Ladder to Edale

The long stony descent eastwards is along the line of the Pennine Way and provides a good prospect over the head of the Vale of Edale. The last steep drop down Jacob's Ladder leads to Yongate Bridge, spanning the young River Noe and is a rare survivor from the packhorse days. This is a typical packhorse bridge, narrow and steeply humped.

The 'ladder' was thought to be the work of Jacob Marshall who, in the eighteenth century, carried wool for Edale farmers over the hills to Stockport, a job called 'bragging'. He constructed steps up the steep track to use as a short cut while the packhorses took a more circuitous

Winter at the head of the Edale Valley.

route leftwards up the paved slabs of the zigzags, past what are now the ruins of Edale Head House where Jacob lived. Jacob's Ladder has been tastefully resurfaced with excellent stonework and the zigzags of the old packhorse way are less used nowadays.

Continuing along the pleasant lane past Lea House, the outlying hamlet of Upper Booth is reached, from where a good field track can be followed across Broadlee Bank, on the lower slopes of Grindslow Knoll, to Edale, the Nag's Head Inn and maybe the train back to Chinley.

Barber Booth to Mount Famine

The walk continues back to Chinley, by heading down the lane towards the hamlet of Barber Booth. Most of the 'booths' in the Edale Valley date back to the sixteenth or seventeenth century and were simple shelters for cattle and sheep and for the herdsmen and shepherds who tended them.

After passing under the railway bridge, a path climbs right across fields near Manor House, to Chapel Gate. This ancient way has for centuries carried travellers over the wild country between Edale and Chapel-en-le-Frith. The track leads up to Rushup Edge from where a broad, grassy ridge is followed north around the head of the Edale Valley, across the peaty watershed of Colborne, passing the ventilator of Cowburn Tunnel seen a short distance to the west and at 275m/900ft, the deepest railway ventilator shaft in England. As you approach Brown Knoll, at 569m/1867ft, the highest point on the circuit, the toppled hills of western Peakland may be seen.

Ahead, a grassy ridge leads west towards the shapely twin tops of Mount Famine and South Head. A rutted track – an old packhorse route linking Hayfield with Tideswell – is eventually joined and it is only a short climb up grassy slopes to the whaleback summit of South Head (494m/1608ft) where you are rewarded by fine views across to Chinley Churn.

INFORMATION
Start/Finish: Station Road, Chinley GR040826.
Distance/Time: 14km(9miles) / 4hours or 22km(14miles) / 7hours.
Grading: Difficult: along tracks and footpaths through hill pastures and over high moorland.
Maps: OS Outdoor Leisure sheet 1 Dark Peak Area and Harveys Superwalker Dark Peak.
Refreshments: Cafés and pubs in Chinley; the Lamb Inn on the Hayfield road just south of Chinley Head; the Nag's Head Inn and Jolly Rambler at Edale.
Public Transport: Buses from Stockport and trains from Manchester and Sheffield.

After descending South Head a faint path can be followed up the summit ridge of the slightly lower Mount Famine (473m/1552ft) from where a vista opens up to the northwest over the walled fields around Southhead Farm and down the Sett Valley, backed by Kinder Bank Woods.

Mount Famine to Chinley

Below Mount Famine's southern ridge, walled grassy paths and tracks descend southwest past Andrews Farm to join the Hayfield to Chapel-en-le-Frith road, beyond which a footpath traverses down fields towards Otter Brook. The stream is easily crossed at a small, gritstone-slabbed bridge from where scrubland leads up to the quiet Maynestone Road, giving a gentle stroll back down into Chinley.

Edale Cross.

A steep track leads down from Edale Cross to Jacob's Ladder.

WALK 27   Edale to the Snake

Edale, set in a shallow, fertile valley at the foot of Peakland's highest upland massif, was mentioned in the Domesday Book and was a place of some importance where five packhorse ways converged. Today, it is an ideal centre for walks and explorations in the Vale of Edale and surrounding hills.

Starting from the village a very challenging walk of the highest quality can be enjoyed across Kinder Scout plateau to Ashop Clough, followed by a climb over the featureless Featherbed Moss to the Snake Road and then turning east along the ancient Doctor's Gate before descending into Lady Clough, in the upper part of the Hope Woodlands Valley. Below the Snake Inn a steady climb allows a second crossing of Kinder Scout on a different line back to Edale. The walk passes through some of the Dark Peak's finest scenery.

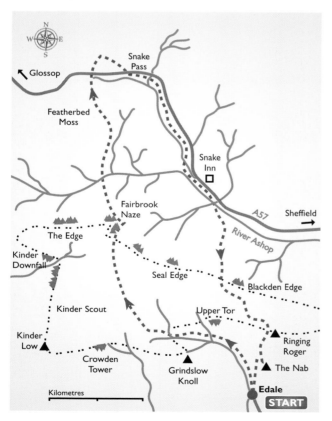

The Mushroom Stone overlooks the head of Grindsbrook Clough.

Edale to Crowden Head.

From the centre of the village, actually called Grindsbrook Booth, a well signposted way leads into the broad entrance of Grindsbrook Clough. This was the original start (or finish) of the Pennine Way and became so popular with walkers that serious erosion developed. This long distance footpath has been re-routed from Edale, west up Jacob's Ladder.

As we go up Grindsbrook Clough the valley narrows, overshadowed by conical Grindslow Knoll to the south and the gritstone escarpments of Nether and Upper Tor to the north. In the upper reaches of the clough the main stream veers off right into the deep gorge below the sheer walls of Grindsbrook Towers, while our route goes straight ahead, up the steep bouldery stream bed onto the plateau and we continue over peat groughs and paths towards the rocky buttresses of Crowden Tower, at the head of Crowden Clough.

From the top of the rocks you can look north to the most challenging part of the walk, a crossing of the Kinder plateau via Crowden Head (629m/2064 feet) to the top of Fairbrook Clough. The walk takes you over a tableland of chocolate-coloured peat, deeply eroded into steep-sided groughs which slow progress. Route finding is often difficult for the first time visitor, even in clear weather, and in mist the experienced bogtrotter is fully tested. This mainly trackless wilderness provides a real feeling of isolation.

Overlooking Ashop Clough, backed by Featherbed Moss and Bleaklow.

Above: *A winter crossing of Kinder Scout.*

Left: *The Old Nag's Head, Edale.*

Crowden Head, at the heart of the Kinder Scout massif, is the great watershed of this part of England; from it the Kinder River drains to the Goyt, Mersey and Irish Sea, while the Noe, Crowden, Grinds, Blackden and Fair Brooks enter the Derwent, Trent and eventually the North Sea.

Fairbrook Naze to Snake Summit.

At the bold prow of Fairbrook Naze, just north of the head of Fairbrook Clough, the deep trench of Ashop Clough lies ahead with Featherbed Moss and the dark outline of Bleaklow filling the skyline beyond. In late summer a carpet of purple heather cloaks these slopes. Running up the opposite side of Ashop Clough is Upper Gate Clough, the next section of the walk. If the weather turns bad or you want to shorten the walk then an easy descent right down the long spur overlooking Fair Brook gives easy access to the Snake Road. The full route, though, descends straight ahead down steep slopes to the River Ashop crossing point beside a ruined shooting cabin. Beyond here there is a change in the vegetation; a natural boundary between the bilberry, heather and crowberry of Kinder Scout, and the acid, often wet, boggy moorlands towards Bleaklow.

A steady climb through Upper Gate Clough and over the desolate Featherbed Moss leads to the A57 Sheffield – Glossop road at the Snake Summit, where the Pennine Way comes in from the southwest. After heading north along the Pennine Way for a short distance, you reach the paved area of the Roman road known as Doctor's Gate. Turning southeast along this ancient packhorse route, built on the line of the Roman road linking Melandra, Glossop with Navio in the Hope Valley, you come down to the A57 road again at Doctor's Gate Culvert.

A short distance along the busy main road east, at a stile on the right, the Lady Clough Forest Trail is joined which runs through the conifers, eventually emerging near the Snake Inn. Originally known as Lady Clough House, the Snake Inn was built in 1821 to serve travellers on Thomas Telford's new road over the Snake Pass and it took its new name from the then Duke of Devonshire, who owned the inn, and part of whose crest was a snake. Today it is a refuge for thirsty walkers.

Snake Inn to Edale.

Just beyond the inn a footpath can be followed down through the conifers on the right to cross the River Ashop by a robust footbridge, and so take to the hill path round into Gate Side Clough up which a path climbs steeply onto the edge path at Seal Stones. An alternative way, and one that passes through some impressive terrain, is to contour round across Wood Moor, and ascend the dramatic rocky valley of Blackden Clough, which provides some great scrambling, once again joining the edge path south of Seal Stones.

Kinder Scout plateau is now crossed to the south at its narrowest point towards Nether Tor high above Grindsbrook. The edge path leads east to the rocky arête of Ringing Roger from where a steep, grassy descent lands you at The Nab. All that now remains is to follow the zigzag track down to Grindsbrook and Edale.

Following a Kinder grough.

INFORMATION
Start/Finish: Grindsbrook Booth (Edale) GR: 123860.
Distance/Time: 19km(12 miles) / 7hours.
Grading: Very difficult; a long walk over peat and heather moorland requiring stamina and good navigational ability, especially in bad weather.
Maps: OS Outdoor Leisure sheet 1 Dark Peak Area and Harveys Superwalker Dark Peak.
Refreshments: Snake Inn and the Old Nag's Head at Edale.
Public Transport: Trains from Stockport and Sheffield to Edale.

BLEAKLOW AND BLACK HILL AREA

Bleaklow is the heartland and high point of the great wilderness of heather moors and gritstone edges lying north of the Snake Pass. It is the largest area in England uncrossed by a road and at its highest point is the 2.5km/1.5mile long broad, east-west watershed reaching 628m/2060ft at Bleaklow Head. This moorland landscape is largely featureless and can be a depressing place in low cloud and heavy rain, when the peat groughs become sticky and navigation can create a few problems. Despite its modest height it is an area not to be underestimated, for in a severe winter, storms often as harsh as anywhere in the higher mountains of England and Wales can occur, making crossing the plateau a serious expedition. Walking on Bleaklow is at its best during periods of severe frost or during drought conditions.

Bleaklow has always been more inaccessible than neighbouring Kinder Scout, and early last century it was the exclusive province of the more experienced ramblers, generally known as 'bogtrotters'. One of the most demanding walks of those early days was the famous Edale to Marsden walk across Kinder, Bleaklow and Black Hill. Even after the setting up in 1951 of the Peak District National Park and the creation of Open Country, it was comparatively rare to see another walking party on the high backbone of Bleaklow or Howden Moors. There was a sense of exploration long after the aloofness of Kinder Scout had been diminished by its popularity. Nowadays the paved sections of the Pennine Way that meander across the moors have made access to this wilderness area much easier.

Separating Bleaklow from Black Hill is Longdendale, the deepest of the Dark Peak's valleys. This dramatic trough cut into the gritstone uplands by the River Etherow and its many short tributaries, now contains a string of five reservoirs built between 1848 and 1877 to supply Manchester and Stockport with drinking water. An important packhorse route ran through Longdendale, used by medieval and later travellers and particularly by salt traders carrying their merchandise from from the Cheshire salt mines across the south Pennines into Yorkshire. Salter's Brook is the name of Etherow's upper reaches and close beside Salter's Brook Bridge, where the thundering traffic on the trans-Pennine route (A628) crosses it, stood the famous Miller's Arms.

Double-headed, steam-hauled trains no longer thrash up the incline to the sooty portals of Woodhead Tunnel, and the grimy turrets of ornate Woodhead railway station have long been demolished. The 5km/3miles long tunnel – one of the longest in the world at that time – linked Manchester with Sheffield via the Etherow and Don valleys. Closed in the early 1980s, the track of the old railway is now part of the recently created Longdendale Trail, a section of the Trans-Pennine route from Liverpool to Hull.

Northwards, beyond Longdendale, rears the mass of gritstone upland culminating in Black Hill (582m/1910ft). It is a huge open area where the dunlin and curlew are kings in summertime and, in early spring, the mountain hare is conspicuous in its changing white coat. On the northwestern flank of this ultimate reach of Peakland are the deep valleys above Greater Manchester; the Chew has the proportions of a Scottish glen and on its rim are the major crags of Dovestones, Wimberry and Ravenstones.

These upthrusts of Carboniferous gritstone and shale on the northwest crest of the Derbyshire Dome offer some of the best walking in the Dark Peak; a wild country of Arctic countenance in winter conditions; a multi-coloured paradise under a summer sky.

Higher Shelf Stones, Bleaklow from the Snake Summit.

WALK 28 Margery Hill and Howden Moors

The high, breezy Howden Moors, enclosing the eastern side of the Upper Derwent Valley, provide a varied and challenging walk crossing a vast area of untamed heather moorland which gives a feeling of space and also excellent views across Bleaklow, into Ewden Dale and over South Yorkshire's surprisingly varied countryside. From the source of the Derwent, among the giant peat hags and boggy drainage channels at Swains Greave, the return journey follows the infant river as it gathers strength from its many upland tributaries. Howden Moors now form part of the extensive National Trust estate.

King's Tree to Margery Hill

Our route starts from the road that winds its way along the shores of the three reservoirs and ends at King's Tree. A sandy track is followed past the site of ancient Ronksley Farm and, after walking through the conifer plantation for 1.2 km/0.75miles, the former ford of Slippery Stones is

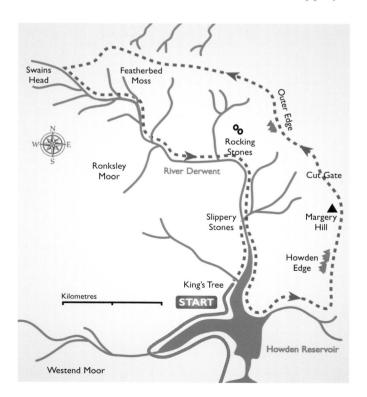

reached which is now spanned by the former Derwent packhorse bridge. This twin-arched bridge, dating from 1683, originally spanned Mill Brook in Derwent Village now submerged in Ladybower Reservoir. In 1682 it was recorded as being the worst of the county's nine bridges needing repairs, the estimated cost being £100! In 1959 it was re-erected stone by stone as a memorial to the late John Derry, champion of early ramblers and author of the classic walkers' guide, *Across the Derbyshire Moors*.

Easy walking southwards along the track on the east bank of Howden Reservoir gives access to the often overlooked Howden Clough, which is climbed for some distance past a small reservoir before ascending east up moorland slopes to Howden Edge and the next objective, Margery Hill's broad, empty summit.

A good path clings to the escarpment of Howden Edge, passing above several crags until eventually Wilfrey Edge is reached and the nearby trig point at the summit of Margery Hill a short distance to the northeast which, at 546m/1791ft, is the highest point in South Yorkshire. Just below Wilfrey Edge is a small gritstone escarpment with a curious hole, known to local inhabitants of a century ago as Wilfrey Neild (Wilfred's Needle) named after the peephole in Saint Wilfred's cell in Ripon Cathedral crypt. Local children used to creep through the hole while the shepherds were gathering their flocks on the surrounding slopes, and in fact the rock marked the boundaries of the respective pastures.

Cut Gate to Swains Head

To the northwest of Margery Hill the moors are crossed by Cut Gate (originally 'Cart Gate'), which has long been used by walkers approaching Howden Moors from the Flouch Inn to the north. For centuries the track was an ancient packhorse route linking the Derwent villages – now submerged – with the market town of Penistone in South Yorkshire. In bad weather this deeply cut trench is a good escape route down to Slippery Stones.

Beyond Cut Gate End, a great sweep of moorland is crossed to the remote trig point at the aptly named Outer Edge (541m/1775ft). From here you can look down to the headwaters of the Derwent. The walk now continues along a boggy path over the featureless terrain of heather and tussocky grass marked by low wooden posts along the watershed between the headwaters of the tributaries draining one way to the Derwent, and the other to the Porter, also known as the Little Don.

Margery Hill and Howden Edge.

An alternative way from Cut Gate End, is to contour on a faint path below the crest of the watershed on the west-facing slopes, to the site of Bull Stones shooting cabins and the walled Lord Edward Howard's Spring. By continuing on this line the outstanding gritstone tors at Crow Stones, with its extremely eroded Rocking Stone, are reached well below Outer Edge, and you can then traverse via Horse Stone Naze into the upper reaches of the Derwent. In high winds this is a route worth considering, because it avoids the higher ground although it is a really good walk in its own right.

Swains Head to King's Tree

From the watershed, a path eventually leads off down to the left over Featherbed Moss to an obvious group of stones known as the Shepherd's Meeting Stones, beyond which the path drops to the eastern banks of the River Derwent just below Swains Head. If the path is difficult to locate then continue round to the broad swampy dip of Swains Head overlooking the hidden depths of Swains Greave, birthplace of the River Derwent and haunt in summer of dunlin and curlew. This area was once aptly described as 'a boggy bowl of utter wilderness'.

After crossing through this wilderness, first a path and later a track, meanders southeast alongside the River Derwent passing within sight of the great Deer Holes landslip. Just before reaching the packhorse bridge at Slippery Stones, a small memorial bridge is crossed, dedicated to the legendary Edale walker, Fred Heardman, a former owner of the Nag's Head Inn. It is now only a short walk back through the forest plantation to the King's Tree.

INFORMATION
Start/Finish: The King's Tree, Upper Derwent Valley GR 168938. On summer weekends and Bank Holidays the valley road is closed to vehicular traffic beyond Fairholmes from where a minibus service operates at these times. At other times access to King's Tree by car is possible.
Distance/Time: 23km(14miles) / 7hours.
Grading: Very difficult; a strenuous high moorland walk where map and compass skills are essential.
Maps: OS Outdoor Leisure sheet 1 Dark Peak Area and Harveys Superwalker Dark Peak.
Refreshments: Fairholmes; the Ladybower Inn and Yorkshire Bridge Inn near Bamford.
Public Transport: Railway station at Bamford. Derwent Valley served by buses from Sheffield and Glossop.

The Upper Derwent Valley from Howden Edge.

The reconstructed packhorse bridge at Slippery Stones.

The Cut Gate path with Outer Edge visible on the skyline.

WALK 29 Bleaklow Stones and Westend Moor

For the serious hill walker, Bleaklow is one of the best places in the Peak District to experience a feeling of remoteness. There is nowhere quite like it; Britain's only true desert and slightly lower than its neighbour, Kinder Scout. A fine approach into this remote wilderness is up the Westend Valley, in the upper reaches of the Derwent Valley, and after crossing the open, tor-dotted plateau of Bleaklow, the eastern rim of Alport Dale, one of the area's major dales, may be descended to Alport Castles, from where easy grassy slopes lead gently back down to the starting point.

Westend to Grinah Stones

This walk starts from the Westend Bridge, situated about 5km/3miles beyond Fairholmes at a sharp bend in the road running through the woods alongside the western arm of Howden Reservoir. From the bridge the way is along a track up through the coniferous plantation beside the River Westend, one of the main

The Westend Valley.

tributaries of the Derwent in the northern section. Beyond the trees the valley opens up, dotted with the remains of the ancient oak, hawthorn and rowan forest.

Some distance away on the moor top at the head of the valley, the bold prow of Grinah Stones is visible looking like some impregnable fortress. The track climbs steeply above Grinah Grain along the broad whaleback of Ridgewalk Moor towards the boulders at Round Hill and beyond the dip to the eroded rocks at Barrow Stones. A brief walk southwest across the moor takes you to the bold, craggy prow of Grinah Stones occupying a remote spur of the Bleaklow plateau. Amongst the eroded boulders are the Sow and Piglet rocks, reminiscent of Ilkley's Cow and Calf rocks in Yorkshire. This is an enchanting place to while away some time, especially on windy days when the boulders provide a sheltered lunch spot. The top of the edge here is at 579m/1900ft and gives broad views over southern Bleaklow to Kinder Scout, while Margery Hill and Derwent Edge are visible to the east. An alternative, and just as enjoyable approach to this bouldery area is via Lynch Clough, which cuts deeply into Ronksley Moor above the King's Tree at the road head of the Upper Derwent.

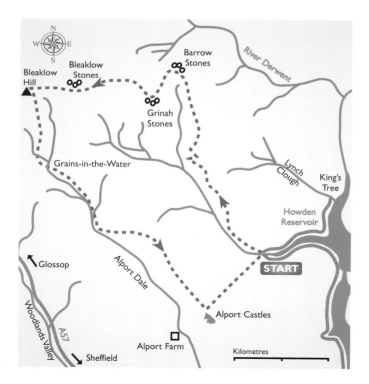

Eroded rocks at Barrow Stones.

Above: *The Anvil Stone at Bleaklow Stones.*

Left: *Bleaklow's wilderness of peat hags and groughs.*

Far left: *Grinah Stones at the head of the Westend Valley.*

Grinah Stones to Grains-in-the-Water

From Grinah Stones a good path contours west around the head of Deep Grain to a jumble of small tors at 628m/2060ft. These are the Bleaklow Stones of which the three-pronged Trident and the wonderfully wind-eroded Anvil Stone are the most impressive. The going along this broad east-west ridge is a mixture of heather, tussocky grasses and boggy peat in places and a keen eye should be kept on the compass, especially in misty conditions when the boundary stakes marking this gentle watershed ridge between streams draining north to the Etherow and those flowing south into the Alport, are useful aids to navigation.

Negotiating the oozing peat and climbing in and out of steep-sided groughs can be tiring work, but is much easier during periods of drought or hard frost. However, in real winter conditions with deep snow it can be a wild and desolate place which demands hill craft skills of the highest order.

Alport Castles.

At Bleaklow Hill our route turns south to pick up the headwaters of the River Alport at Alport Head. Here, the first drops of this major river are collected in a great expanse of bare peat and gritty debris. From Alport Head, open heather moorland cut by numerous streams leads south down to the broad, wet hollow aptly known as The Swamp. Where the young Alport is joined by the stream in Hern Clough lies the lovely Grains-in-the-Water, first recorded in 1840, it means 'the forking of rivers'. This is a fine tranquil place in the wide bowl of surrounding hills and in spring you can rest here and listen to the call of skylarks, and the flutey song of the golden plover. The nearby conurbations of Manchester and Sheffield could be a million miles away.

Grains-in-the-Water to Howden Reservoir

Ahead is the deeply cut and sinuous Alport Dale. A path, faint at first, takes you through the fascinating section below Grains-in-the-Water, with rock pools, waterslides, stretches of bedrock and the two fine waterfalls, in miniature rocky gorges between Grindlesgrain Tor and Glethering Clough, which are among the best in the area. Near Glethering Clough, which means 'sheep gathering', a path slants up to the valley rim and then descends gently past the isolated Alport trig point. The edge path continues to the huge landslip of Alport Castles with its crumbling cliffs of gritstone and shale rearing up above the hamlet of Alport far below by the winding river.

After a last look up the full sweep of Alport Dale backed by Bleaklow's broad summit ridge, the high ground is quitted for a path to the north-east slanting steadily down the moor towards the mouth of the Westend Valley and the mature trees of Ditch Clough Plantation, not far from our starting point.

INFORMATION

Start/Finish: The Westend Bridge, upper Derwent Valley GR154927. On summer weekends and Bank Holidays the valley road is closed to vehicular traffic beyond Fairholmes from where a minibus service operates at these times.

Distance/Time: 18km(11miles) / 6hours.

Grading: Very difficult; a demanding walk across Bleaklow's high moorland plateau. Crossing the boggy, peat-hagged terrain can be difficult during bad weather.

Maps: OS Outdoor Leisure sheet 1 Dark Peak Area and Harveys Superwalker Dark Peak.

Refreshments: Fairholmes; the Ladybower Inn and Yorkshire Bridge Inn near Bamford.

Public Transport: Railway station at Bamford. Derwent Valley served by buses from Sheffield and Glossop.

Waterfall in the upper reaches of Alport Dale.

The narrows of Alport Dale backed by Bleaklow.

Bleaklow Stones.

WALK 30 Higher Shelf Stones and Bleaklow Head

When walkers think of wild, lonely and often inhospitable Bleaklow, images arise of oozing peat bogs, hags and deep groughs from which escape can be quite a struggle. The moor has few landmarks and it is has been referred to as Britain's only true desert. Yet there is nowhere else quite like it.

Bleaklow is a very special place and, despite the summit dome having no dramatic shape, when seen from the west the moors look quite rugged, especially the sharp profile of Higher Shelf Stones. The view from Higher Shelf Stones is arguably one of the finest in the northern Peak District and this vantage point is visited during a circular walk starting from Old Glossop, crossing to Bleaklow Head and then returning along the deep rim of the clough high above Yellowslacks Brook.

Glossop to Higher Shelf Stones

The town of Glossop developed rapidly during the Industrial Revolution when cotton mills played a major part in its economy. Fortunately, the original medieval settlement of Old Glossop survived and its tiny

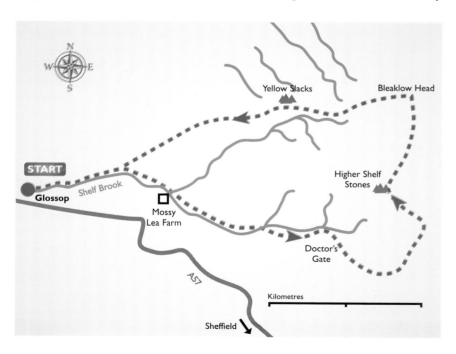

market square, with detached stone cottages clustered around the parish church, provides a pleasant starting point for our walk.

From All Saint's church, the walk passes the old cross and turns left along Shepley Street to join a track leading eastwards towards Mossy Lea (or Mossylee) Farm. The track crosses Yellowslacks Brook near the farm and then climbs steadily up the valley of the Shelf Brook. This ancient trackway marked as Doctor's Gate on the map, has been known by this name for at least 350 years and was named after Dr John Talbot – the illegitimate son of the Earl of Shrewsbury – who was vicar of Glossop from 1494 to 1550. He is known to have often travelled this way in pre-turnpike days to visit his father's castle in Sheffield.

Doctor's Gate – 'gate' is an old Norse word for road or track – is also shown as a Roman Road on the OS map, possibly linking the forts at Melandra near Glossop, and Navio, at Brough in the Hope Valley. However, the stones on this track are probably from a medieval pack-horse route connecting Glossop with the Woodlands Valley beyond the Snake Summit. Whatever its origins, the track gives pleasant walking and after passing a large cairn above the steep zigzags of Urchin Clough you eventually join the paved section of the Pennine Way, weaving its way across the boggy terrain just north of the Snake Summit.

An alternative way is to leave Doctor's Gate at the cairn and follow an edge path along the eastern flank of Crooked Clough which runs parallel with the Pennine Way. As you traverse the rim of the clough you get an excellent view across to the mountain-like Higher Shelf Stones which dominate the scene and can be approached directly from just beyond a picturesque rocky gorge and waterfall. Here, in spring, you are likely to see mountain hares, still with their white winter coats, scampering across the grassy slopes below the summit rocks.

On a clear day from beside the triangulation point at this often breezy promenade with its graffiti-covered boulders (much of which dates back to the beginning of the nineteenth century), you can look over Coldharbour Moors to the northern flanks of Kinder Scout, and to its right, Mill Hill, Chinley Churn and the distant hills of the Goyt. To the north, beyond the Longdendale Valley, you can pick out Laddow Rocks backed by Black Hill. Just east of the summit a US Air Force B29 Superfortress crashed, killing all 13 crew members. Large pieces of wreckage are still scattered about on the slopes.

Heading for Bleaklow Head from Higher Shelf Stones.

Higher Shelf Stones to Bleaklow Head

To the north of Higher Shelf Stones lies a vast landscape of peat hags and heather, cut by deep groughs. By heading along the broad ridge through a morass of peat groughs, you pass the eroded Hern Stones, and continue along to the Wain Stones at Bleaklow Head, which, at 633m/2076feet, is the second highest summit in the Peak District. After periods of heavy rain and in poor visibilty, good navigation is essential along this stretch of wet, boggy moorland.

This is the great watershed of England, its streams eventually draining to the Irish Sea, via the Mersey, and the North Sea, via the Humber. John Hillaby, in his book *Journey Through Britain*, described this peaty ocean as being 'extraordinarily depressing'. Don't be put off, for the openness and freedom of Bleaklow has few rivals.

Prior to the 1950s there was no freedom of access here and Bleaklow was strictly private, the only routes being a few shooter's ways up from the valley. Nowadays, especially at summer weekends, you may share the summit boulders at Bleaklow Head with groups of Pennine Wayfarers.

Wain Stones to Glossop

From the boulders of the Wain Stones you now turn southwest, and cross Shelf Moss by a series of wide groughs leading to the head of Dowstone Clough. The clough soon leads into the deeply-cut ravine of Yellowslacks Brook, whose northern rim can be followed down a broad ridge.

There are few gritstone outcrops on Bleaklow, and the only major one on its western flanks is Yellow Slacks which you pass during the descent. The crag has a troubled history, when in the early 1960s a local farmer tried to blow up the rocks with explosives in an attempt to keep climbers away. Fortunately he failed, and now climbers and walkers are able to appreciate the splendid vista from the escarpment into the depths of the rugged valley of Yellowslacks Brook which contains a fine waterfall.

By continuing down grassy Lightside Ridge, overlooking the unusually-named Shittern Clough on the right of its lower slopes, you rejoin the outward route opposite the partially wooded dome of Shire Hill. Turning right the track soon leads back into Old Glossop.

Eroded boulders at Higher Shelf Stones.

Approaching the summit of Doctor's Gate from Glossop.

INFORMATION
Start/Finish: Old Glossop GR 042948.
Distance/Time: 14km(9 miles) / 6hours.
Grading: Very difficult; a high level walk mainly along paths but including some boggy moorland. Good navigational skills required.
Maps: OS Outdoor Leisure sheet 1 Dark Peak Area and Harveys Superwalker Dark Peak .
Refreshments: Pubs and cafés in Glossop.
Public Transport: Regular bus service from Manchester and surrounding towns.

The summit of Higher Shelf Stones.

WALK 31 Longdendale and Bleaklow's Northern Edges

Above Longdendale the vast and desolate moorland areas of Bleaklow and Black Hill are fringed by a line of dramatic gritstone outcrops, forming a serrated skyline cut by a series of impressive cloughs that carry streams down to join the River Etherow. Starting from the hamlet of Crowden this circular walk traverses the rim of Longdendale's craggy moorland skyline and provides great vantage points for views across to Black Hill and Bleaklow.

Longdendale's chain of five reservoirs was once the largest area of artificial water in the world and sadly, as in other parts of the south Pennines, reservoir building resulted in the destruction of old mills, scattered farms and part of the village of Crowden. Here stood the old Crowden Hall, home of the Hatfields for generations and demolished in 1937 by Manchester Corporation. Close beside the mouth of Crowden Great Clough is the Rotherham Outdoor Centre, and nearby the last remaining terraced cottages, known as Long Row, were converted by the National Park into a popular youth hostel. Crowden also once had its own railway station on the Woodhead line across the valley.

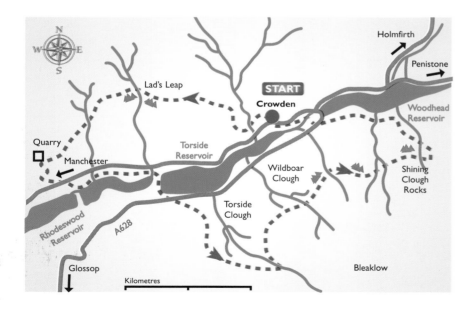

Traversing the rim of Lad's Leap. Bleaklow is visible across Longdendale.

Crowden to Torside Clough

Leaving the car park and passing the camp site – built where the former Crowden Hall stood – a walled lane leads left crossing the Crowden Brook Bridge to join the Pennine Way, whose track is followed north. The track is soon quitted at a ladder stile for a path climbing left out of the Crowden valley and crosses open heather moorland above Highstone Rocks to reach Lad's Leap. Here, the Hollins Clough stream tumbles down slabby bed rocks and after heavy rain, and with strong southwesterlies, blows back onto the moors – a sort of mini Kinder Downfall.

Beyond the clough a narrow path leads along the edge of Millstone Rocks and continues along the brim of the moor, a peaty path crosses Black Gutter, passing a series of posts alongside an old water pipe. Another path drops down left by Rawkins Brook to the impressive Tintwistle Knarr Quarry, where an old quarry track slants rightwards through the woods of Didsbury Intake. A series of zigzags eventually lead down through grass and heather to the main Woodhead Pass road.

The upper reaches of Torside Clough, Black Hill in the distance.

Shining Clough Rocks.

Across the road to the left a tarmaced lane drops down through woodland to Rhodeswood Dam, from where a permissive path heads eastwards through scrubland overlooking the reservoir. The path eventually comes out on the north side of Torside Reservoir dam wall which is crossed to a lane leading up to where the Longdendale Trail meets a road. Straight ahead a track leads to Reaps Farm above which you follow the Pennine Way along the path climbing up to Clough Edge, from where you can gaze into the gloomy, rocky depths of Torside Clough.

Torside Clough to Shining Clough

As the head of the clough closes in, just south of the spring at John Track Well, you need to cross the stream and contour northwest round the edge of the untracked Sykes Moor, aiming for Torside Naze. The moorland edge, with its patches of bare peat and scattered boulders, eventually swings round into the upper reaches of the rocky ravine of Wildboar Clough. A wire fence, which guards the entrance to Wildboar Clough, can be followed to an appropriate crossing point leading back along the opposite side.

In very wet weather care is needed crossing the clough. However, in dry conditions, an ascent of Wildboar Clough as part of an approach route to Bleaklow Head is considered one of the best gritstone scrambles in the Peak. The bed of the clough is a grand gully with convenient rock steps and slabs separating little pools and water trickles in fine positions between impending rock faces. The higher you go the better the view across to Crowden Great Brook, with Laddow Rocks perched on its rim and the dome of Black Hill in the far distance.

After crossing Wildboar Clough, a faint path now veers right above the jumbled rocks and craggy walls of the Rollick Stones, the line becoming more prominent beyond Fair Vage Clough. The path contours eastwards where moorland meets the craggy, gritstone promenade of Lawrence Edge and Deer Knowl overlooking Woodhead Reservoir, finally traversing around the deep and rocky headwall of Shining Clough. Here the water rushes down over steps of rock and care is needed at the crossing when the steam is in spate.

Once across, the path traverses the opposite banks of the clough back to the edge and the impressive buttresses of Dowstone Rocks. First explored in the early 1920s, these rocks are known as Shining Clough Rocks, and are worth a closer look. The exposed crags offer some of the most challenging and imposing buttresses in the Dark Peak although, in recent years, parts of the crag have tumbled down the hillside.

174

Shining Clough to Crowden

Continuing beyond the rocks to Stable Clough, a fence is followed uphill to a shooter's track that traverses below the Shining Clough Rocks. After crossing rough terrain you eventually join the pleasantly wooded Shining Clough brook where an obvious path now descends past a pond until a narrow track takes you down to the access road leading to The Lodge.

As you amble left along the track, past the old red brick cottages of Crowden's tiny railway station which closed in 1957, you eventually arrive at the road. Just left of here you head right down through woodland to a footbridge over the Etherow beneath the Woodhead dam wall. The way back to Crowden follows the permissive footpath west across the grassy slopes overlooking Torside Reservoir backed by Bleaklow's edges, maybe with their buttresses picked out by the sun's slanting rays as it dips to the west.

INFORMATION
Start/Finish: Car park at Crowden GR 073994.
Distance/Time: 18km(11miles) / 6hours.
Grading: Difficult; a strenuous, high level moorland and edge path walk. Skills in map and compass work essential.
Maps: OS Outdoor Leisure sheet 1 Dark Peak Area and Harveys Superwalker Dark Peak.
Refreshments: Crowden.
Public Transport: National Express bus from Sheffield and Manchester.

Above: *Scrambling up Wildboar Clough.*

Left: *Traversing around the upper reaches of Wildboar Clough.*

175

WALK 32 Laddow and Black Hill

To the north of Longdendale lies a wild landscape of open moorland through which the Pennine Way passes, crossing the highest point of the plateau at Black Hill – real bogtrotting terrain. By starting from Crowden, and following a horseshoe circuit around the little used moors overlooking Crowden Little Brook to Black Hill's summit, then returning via the belvedere of Laddow Rocks high above Crowden Great Brook, an excellent moorland outing can be enjoyed with some great views to broad horizons.

Crowden to Black Hill

Starting from the car park, you head past the campsite to join a track heading up the valley on the right. The track soon leads to a path climbing north up grass and bracken-covered slopes, above the oak and birch trees of the Brockholes Nature Reserve, and then past the disused Brockholes and Loftend Quarries. At its peak, Loftend Quarry, also known as Crowden Great Quarry, was the largest in the area, and employed over a hundred men, while today, its steep, south-facing gritstone walls and corners provide challenges to rock climbers.

Above the quarries the path climbs the ridge to the summit of Hey Moss then continues up the broad, moorland ridge high above Crowden Little Brook. Here you can look back across Torside Reservoir to the crag-rimmed heights of Bleaklow filling the southern skyline, while in the distance to the left you can pick out the Woodhead Pass road climbing out of the valley. Ahead now lies Westend Moss – with a little reedy pool on its summit plateau – and the broad heather ridge leading to White Low. The broad shoulder of Tooleyshaw Moss is crossed by a thin path weaving its way through an area of grough channels, peat hags and boggy ground past some cairns to Black Hill.

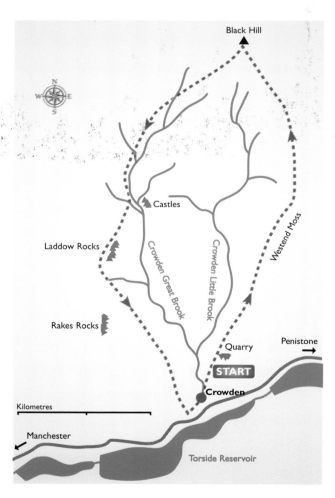

Crowden-in-Longdendale.

At (582m/1908ft), and formerly the highest point of the old county of Cheshire, Black Hill is appropriately named. It really is black and the crossing of this squelchy summit area has been notorious for years, especially after periods of heavy rain. Wainwright described the place as a 'desolate and hopeless quagmire; peat, naked and unashamed!', while John Hillaby likened it to a 'monstrous chocolate cake of peat ringed by the candle-like heads of cotton grass'. However, the place does have a fascinating attraction to keen moorland walkers.

The summit of Black Hill is also known as Soldier's Lump from the early surveying days. In 1841 a wooden framework of a huge Great Ramsden theodolite, set up in 1784 as part of the original triangulation of the country, was found. Its site is now occupied by the concrete triangulation pillar standing high above the level of the surrounding peat, and the original theodolite is now in the Science Museum.

The broad summit of Black Hill prevents good views into the many valleys and cloughs which run up towards it, but you can pick out Laddow Rocks, which we visit on the next stage of the walk, while east, is the Holme Moss television mast with its flashing warning lights.

Black Hill to Laddow

Our way now lies southwest along the Pennine Way. In recent years the erosion along this section through some very fragile, boggy territory had become so bad that the National Park Authority laid a solid, stone pathway right up to Black Hill's peaty summit. No matter how you view this constructed path, it has certainly eased the passage for weary Pennine Way walkers and should, in the long term, reduce much of the worst erosion.

From Black Hill the path crosses moorland to Dun Hill, then gradually descends across Grains Moss to the twin rocky outcrops of The Castles overlooking Crowden Great Brook and defending the head of the valley. A gentle ascent up the western rim of the moor, above the deeply cut clough, lands you at the start of Laddow Rocks.

Laddow to Crowden

Laddow's steep buttresses of fairly coarse millstone grit are situated in a very exposed position overlooking Crowden Great Brook, and were some of the first rocks to be explored by Manchester climbers as early as 1901. As such they hold an important place in the history of rock climbing in the Peak District. Another historic, though unfortunate event occurred here in 1928, which led to the eventual

Crowden Great Brook.

Laddow Rocks.

formation of the Mountain Rescue Committee in 1933. A climber was knocked off one of the climbs and seriously injured. Using a makeshift stretcher, made from two 'Trespassers will be Prosecuted' signposts, a difficult rescue ensued and the casualty was eventually evacuated down to Crowden. The incident was also responsible for the formation of the Joint Stretcher Committee leading to the design of the famous Thomas stretcher, which was to occupy many of the rescue stations in the hills throughout England and Wales. Mountain rescue is now run by the Peak District Mountain Rescue Organisation and involves six teams spread throughout the National Park.

The descent from Laddow to Crowden follows the moorland rim path, crosses picturesque Oakenclough Brook and gradually descends below Rakes Rocks and Black Tor, accompanied by pleasant views down to the Longdendale reservoirs with Bleaklow frowning over them. A track is finally reached that can be followed left over Crowden Brook Bridge back to the hamlet.

Above: *Perfect snow conditions on Westend Moss.*

Right: *The valley of Crowden Great Brook backed by Black Hill.*

INFORMATION
Start/Finish: Crowden GR073994.
Distance/Time: 14km(9miles) / 5hours.
Grading: Difficult; a strenuous moorland walk sometimes on unclear paths. Good map and compass work essential.
Maps: OS Outdoor Leisure sheet 1 Dark Peak Area and Harveys Superwalker Dark Peak.
Refreshments: At Crowden.
Public Transport: National Express bus from Manchester and Sheffield.

WALK 33 Chew Valley and the Saddleworth Edges

In the northwest corner of the Peak District National Park, to the west of Black Hill, lies an area of wild moorland fringed by the rocky escarpments of Saddleworth's Chew Valley. From these lofty edges you can look down on the sparkling waters of a chain of reservoirs above the village of Greenfield and beyond to the Tame valley and the sprawling outskirts of Greater Manchester. The area was once the heart of a thriving textile industry with numerous mills and rows of workers' terraced cottages dotted along the valley floor but as with much of Britain's textile industry, most of the mills are long gone.

This circular walk starts at the car park at Dovestone Reservoir and involves a stroll alongside three dams, before traversing the gritstone edges of Saddleworth Moor, finally returning along the moorland rim of the spectacular Chew Valley. Since pre-war days the Saddleworth Moors have been the domain of northern ramblers or bogtrotters and our walk follows in their footsteps.

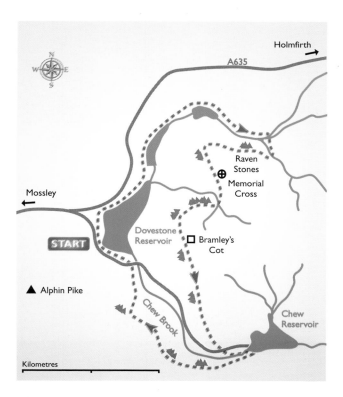

The Trinnacle, Raven Stones.

Despite the popularity of this mini-Lakeland, most visitors remain close to the car parks, beside the relatively modern Dovestone Reservoir where, especially on breezy days, sailing dinghies are often seen racing across its surface, their bright sails adding a touch of colour to the dark surroundings.

Dovestone Reservoir to Ravenstones

From the car park a good track is followed along the western edges of the Dovestone, Yeoman Hey and Greenfield Reservoirs passing below the wooded slopes of Bill o'Jacks Plantation overlooked by the site of the old Moor Cock Inn. Like many hill pubs in the area which provided refreshments for thirsty pre-war ramblers, it has long since gone. On the opposite side of Dovestone Reservoir's northern tip lie the ruins of Ashway Gap House. Constructed in 1850 as a hunting lodge for John Platt, the building served as a hospital during the First World War and as a prisoner of war camp in the Second. The owner's brother, James Platt, then MP for Oldham, died here after a shooting accident on the hills in 1857, the event being recorded by a memorial cross on the moors which is passed on the walk.

Holme Clough and Saddleworth Moors.

Beyond Greenfield Reservoir the scene changes as the track climbs steadily up a rocky defile to the junction between Holme Clough and Birchen Clough, whose waters rise on the featureless plateau of Black Hill before rushing down to fill the chain of reservoirs. The bouldery bed of Birchen Clough offers some pleasant scrambling, particularly in the area of a delightful waterfall. Beyond the falls the stream bed is left for the steep slopes that lead up to the moorland edge path and the start of the most entertaining section of the walk.

The first of many rocky escarpments to be passed is Raven Stones, which sits on a jutting prow in a commanding position set high above steep scree slopes and offers fine views across the broad Saddleworth Moors cut into by the impressive Holme Clough, whose steep-sided slopes of grass and scree give it the appearance of a miniature version of a Cairngorm glen. It was Patrick Monkhouse, celebrated mountain walker and guidebook writer, who in the early 1930s evocatively captured the essence of this area in his book *On Foot in the Peak* when he wrote, 'Look long. You will not often see the moors composed in an outlook so powerful, so sombre or so finely proportioned as this.' Fine sentiments and ones with which many walkers will agree as they take in the view along Saddleworth's edges.

Apart from the views, the Ravenstones were supposedly the last known site of golden eagles in this part of the Pennines, and the eighteenth-century writer Samuel Bottomley wrote of the 'famed Raven Stones':

> There on a cliff, dark frowning to the eye,
> Imperial Eagles build their nests on high.

The other attraction here is the detached three-pronged pinnacle known as the Trinnacle. Although steeply guarded on three sides a short, rocky neck connecting the hillside gives an easy but exposed ascent up to its high point. The place is a great delight for photographers, and friends can usually be persuaded to scramble up its short side and step precariously across the prongs.

Ravenstones to Chew Reservoir

The edge path now continues west along the rocky top of Raven Stones Brow to Ashway Rocks where you can gaze out over Yeoman Hey Reservoir to Dick Hill which provides one of the finest viewpoints in the district. Leaving the rocks behind a narrow path leads up to Ashway Cross, James Platt's blackened memorial supported by two metal rods and looking very out of place in its wild moorland setting.

This is a popular area for memorials for, as you look along across the head of Dovestone Clough, Alderman's Hill can be seen backed by the prominent parish war memorial obelisk at the summit of Pots and Pans – named after the hollows in the gritstone boulders near its top. On the other side of the clough, near the rocky outcrops above Great Dove Stone Rocks, is a conspicuous cairn sitting on a craggy plinth, a memorial to two local climbers who were killed in a mountaineering accident in the Italian Dolomites.

A short distance beyond the cairn stands Bramley's Cot, an old stone shooting cabin which incorporates part of the natural crag into its walls and can provide a good shelter for a snack when the prevailing westerlies sweep their rain across the hillside. Beyond the shelter, the path traverses the edge overlooking the steep gorge through which Chew Brook has carved its way.

Traversing the edge path to Stable Stones Brow.

Chew Brook to Dovestone Reservoir

This is unquestionably one of the Peak District's deepest and most dramatic valleys with its head blocked by the impounding wall of Chew Reservoir, a saucer-like dam surrounded by hummocks of peaty moss, which at 488m/1601ft above sea level is one of the highest in the country. The stretch of water is fringed with cotton grass in summer and provides a sanctuary for moorland birds.

On the southern rim of Chew Valley's steep slopes are dotted numerous outcrops overlooking Chew Brook, and the dam service road which gives an easy way back down into the valley. A more interesting way is to continue along the narrow path that clings to the very edge of the valley rim. The route passes Stable Stones Brow and then continues to the impressive Wimberry Rocks from where you can look across a peaty desert to the splendid viewpoint of Alphin Pike.

From Wimberry Rocks a steep descent over boulders leads to a path through the woodland of Chew Piece Plantation, where the track is eventually joined that takes you back to the car park. The steep quarried faces of Great Dove Stone Rocks, overlooking the reservoir, are a reminder of just how rugged is this corner of the Peak District.

INFORMATION
Start/Finish: Dovestone Reservoir car park GR 013036.
Distance/Time: 13km(8 miles) / 5hours.
Grading: Difficult; along moorland edge paths.
Maps: OS Outdoor Leisure sheet 1 Dark Peak Area and Harveys Superwalker Dark Peak.
Refreshments: Various pubs and cafés in Greenfield.
Public Transport: Buses from Manchester and Oldham to Greenfield; trains from Manchester to local stations.

Waterfall high in Birchen Clough.

PHOTOGRAPHIC NOTES AND AUTHORS' ACKNOWLEDGEMENTS

The photographs for the book were taken over a number of years using a range of equipment including a Hassleblad 503CW 6X6cm, Bronica ETRSi 6X4.5cm, Fuji GSW690 Professional 6x9cm and a Leica R6 35mm, a wide range of different focal length lenses, plus a Sekonic L-508 Zoom Master lightmeter, Manfrotto carbon fibre and Benbo tripods.

Professional Fuji film was mainly used including Fujichrome Velvia, Provia and Sensia. Very few filters were used apart from skylight 1A, circular polariser to intensify cloud patterns, graduated neutral density filter and 81A warming filter. Occasional use was made of an 8x neutral density filter for long exposures of flowing water.

The choice of an anti-clockwise or clockwise circuit of a walk was often governed by the direction of the sunlight at the best viewpoints, but despite careful planning, poor weather conditions often necessitated several visits to get the best lighting. In order to capture the special mood and atmosphere of the landscape some of the photographs were taken in the magic light around dawn and dusk.

Hopefully, the extra effort involved in carrying a heavy tripod and camera equipment has been worthwhile, and the pictures have managed to encapsulate the essence of the White and Dark Peak.

Jerry Rawson

The authors would like to acknowledge the help and support from Katy Rawson with proof reading, art work and maps and also a very big thank you to Roly Smith, editorial manager for Halsgrove and president of the Outdoor Writers' Guild, for his support and invaluable editorial help. The photographer would also like to thank all the friends and strangers alike who patiently posed for photographs.